D0426735

Presented to

By

On the Occasion of

Date

THE BIBLE PROMISE BOOK

NEW LIFE VERSION

ISBN 978-1-59789-682-5

Wherever * is seen, the words that follow are not in all the early writings of the New Testament. If part of a verse or more than one verse is missing in some of the early writings, it is marked [*].

Cover design by Studio Gearbox, www.studiogearbox.com

Published by Barbour Publishing, Inc., P.O. Box 719, Uhrichsville, Ohio 44683, www.barbourbooks.com

Our mission is to publish and distribute inspirational products offering exceptional value and biblical encouragement to the masses.

Printed in China.

5 4 3

Introduction

Our world sends many conflicting signals on the important issues of life. How should we approach anger? Is discipline a good thing or not? Why speak with honesty? Is prayer for real? What is true wisdom?

In His kindness, God has answered all of these questions—and many more—in the pages of His Word, the Bible. Whatever our needs, we can find in scripture the principles we need to address the issues we face.

This collection of Bible verses is a handy reference to some of the key issues that all people—and especially women—face. In these pages, you'll find carefully selected verses that address topics like comfort, encouragement, friendship, purity, rest, and understanding. In fact, more than four dozen categories are covered, arranged alphabetically for ease of use.

This book is not intended to replace regular, personal Bible study. Nor is it a replacement for a good concordance for in-depth study of a particular subject. It is, however, a quick reference to some of the key issues of life that women most often face. We hope it will be an encouragement to you as you read.

All scripture is taken from the New Life Version of the Bible.

Contents

Adversity

Our Creator never intended that we should shoulder a load of suffering ourselves. That's the whole purpose of spiritual community.
Linda Bartlett

I am sure that our suffering now cannot be compared to the shining-greatness that He is going to give us.
Romans 8:18

As we have suffered much for Christ and have shared in His pain, we also share His great comfort. But if we are in trouble, it is for your good. And it is so you will be saved from the punishment of sin. If God comforts us, it is for your good also. You too will be given strength not to give up when you have the same kind of trouble we have.
2 Corinthians 1:5–6

"I have told you these things so you may have peace in Me. In the world you will have much trouble. But take hope! I have power over the world!"
John 16:33

But I gave up those things that were so important to me for Christ. Even more than that, I think of everything as worth nothing. It is so much better to know Christ Jesus my Lord. I have lost everything for Him. And I think of these things as worth nothing so that I can have Christ. . . . I want to know Him. I want to have the same power in my life that raised Jesus from the dead. I want to understand and have a share in His sufferings and be like Christ in His death. Then I may be raised up from among the dead.

PHILIPPIANS 3:7–8, 10–11

These tests have come to prove your faith and to show that it is good. Gold, which can be destroyed, is tested by fire. Your faith is worth much more than gold and it must be tested also. Then your faith will bring thanks and shining-greatness and honor to Jesus Christ when He comes again.

1 PETER 1:7

Those who are right with the Lord cry, and He hears them. And He takes them from all their troubles.

PSALM 34:17

After you have suffered for awhile, God Himself will make you perfect. He will keep you in the right way. He will give you strength. He is the God of all loving-favor and has called you through Christ Jesus to share His shining-greatness forever.

1 PETER 5:10

You are happy when men hate you and do not want you around and put shame on you because you trust in Me.

LUKE 6:22

Is anyone among you suffering? He should pray. Is anyone happy? He should sing songs of thanks to God.

JAMES 5:13

Yes! All who want to live a God-like life who belong to Christ Jesus will suffer from others.

2 TIMOTHY 3:12

Dear friends, your faith is going to be tested as if it were going through fire. Do not be surprised at this. Be happy that you are able to share some of the suffering of Christ. When His shining-greatness is shown, you will be filled with much joy. If men speak bad of you because you are a Christian, you will be happy because the Spirit of shining-greatness and of God is in you.

1 PETER 4:12–14

The little troubles we suffer now for a short time are making us ready for the great things God is going to give us forever.

2 CORINTHIANS 4:17

If we suffer and stay true to Him, then we will be a leader with Him. If we say we do not know Him, He will say He does not know us.

2 TIMOTHY 2:12

This shows you have received loving-favor when you are even punished for doing what is right because of your trust in God. These things are all a part of the Christian life to which you have been called. Christ suffered for us. This shows us we are to follow in His steps. He never sinned. No lie or bad talk ever came from His lips. When people spoke against Him, He never spoke back. When He suffered from what people did to Him, He did not try to pay them back. He left it in the hands of the One Who is always right in judging.

1 PETER 2:19, 21–23

ANGER

Being angry or unforgiving makes it impossible to have a gentle and quiet spirit.
DARLENE WILKINSON

He who is slow to get angry has great understanding, but he who has a quick temper makes his foolish way look right.

PROVERBS 14:29

My Christian brothers, you know everyone should listen much and speak little. He should be slow to become angry. A man's anger does not allow him to be right with God.

JAMES 1:19–20

Do not have anything to do with a man given to anger, or go with a man who has a bad temper. Or you might learn his ways and get yourself into a trap.

PROVERBS 22:24–25

Do not be quick in spirit to be angry. For anger is in the heart of fools.

ECCLESIASTES 7:9

It is better to live in a desert land than with a woman who argues and causes trouble.

PROVERBS 21:19

A gentle answer turns away anger, but a sharp word causes anger.

PROVERBS 15:1

Do all things without arguing and talking about how you wish you did not have to do them.

PHILIPPIANS 2:14

"But I tell you that whoever is angry with his brother will be guilty and have to suffer for his wrong-doing. Whoever says to his brother, 'You have no brains,' will have to stand in front of the court. Whoever says, 'You fool,' will be sent to the fire of hell."

MATTHEW 5:22

A man with a bad temper starts fights, but he who is slow to anger quiets fighting.

PROVERBS 15:18

He who is slow to anger is better than the powerful. And he who rules his spirit is better than he who takes a city.

PROVERBS 16:32

Christian brothers, never pay back someone for the bad he has done to you. Let the anger of God take care of the other person. The Holy Writings say, "I will pay back to them what they should get, says the Lord." (Deuteronomy 32:35)

ROMANS 12:19

A dry piece of food with peace and quiet is better than a house full of food with fighting.

PROVERBS 17:1

If you are angry, do not let it become sin. Get over your anger before the day is finished.

EPHESIANS 4:26

COMFORT

All you really need is the One who promised never to leave or forsake you—the One who said, "Lo, I am with you always."
JONI EARECKSON TADA

Yes, even if I walk through the valley of the shadow of death, I will not be afraid of anything, because You are with me. You have a walking stick with which to guide and one with which to help. These comfort me.

PSALM 23:4

"God will take away all their tears. There will be no more death or sorrow or crying or pain. All the old things have passed away."

REVELATION 21:4

He will take away death for all time. The Lord God will dry tears from all faces. He will take away the shame of His people from all the earth. For the Lord has spoken.

Isaiah 25:8

For the Lord Himself will come down from heaven with a loud call. The head angel will speak with a loud voice. God's horn will give its sounds. First, those who belong to Christ will come out of their graves to meet the Lord. Then, those of us who are still living here on earth will be gathered together with them in the clouds. We will meet the Lord in the sky and be with Him forever. Because of this, comfort each other with these words.

1 Thessalonians 4:16–18

Give all your worries to Him because He cares for you.

1 Peter 5:7

"Comfort, comfort My people," says your God.

Isaiah 40:1

When my worry is great within me, Your comfort brings joy to my soul.

Psalm 94:19

"Those who have sorrow are happy, because they will be comforted."

Matthew 5:4

"Then I will ask My Father and He will give you another Helper. He will be with you forever."

John 14:16

The Spirit of the Lord God is on me, because the Lord has chosen me to bring good news to poor people. He has sent me to heal those with a sad heart. He has sent me to tell those who are being held and those in prison that they can go free. He has sent me to tell about the year of the Lord's favor, and the day our God will bring punishment. He has sent me to comfort all who are filled with sorrow.

Isaiah 61:1–2

"And I am with you always, even to the end of the world."

Matthew 28:20

We give thanks to the God and Father of our Lord Jesus Christ. He is our Father Who shows us loving-kindness and our God Who gives us comfort. He gives us comfort in all our troubles. Then we can comfort other people who have the same troubles. We give the same kind of comfort God gives us. As we have suffered much for Christ and have shared in His pain, we also share His great comfort.

2 Corinthians 1:3–5

"I will not leave you without help as children without parents. I will come to you."

John 14:18

"Come to Me, all of you who work and have heavy loads. I will give you rest."

Matthew 11:28

God is our safe place and our strength. He is always our help when we are in trouble. So we will not be afraid, even if the earth is shaken and the mountains fall into the center of the sea, and even if its waters go wild with storm and the mountains shake with its action.

PSALM 46:1–3

I have remembered Your Law from a long time ago, O Lord, and I am comforted.

PSALM 119:52

"I will comfort you as one is comforted by his mother. And you will be comforted in Jerusalem."

ISAIAH 66:13

Be comforted. Work to get along with others. Live in peace. The God of love and peace will be with you.

2 CORINTHIANS 13:11

Come close to God and He will come close to you.

JAMES 4:8

CONVERSATION

Kind words can be short and easy to speak,
but their echoes are truly endless.
MOTHER TERESA

The tongue is also a small part of the body, but it can speak big things. See how a very small fire can set many trees on fire.

JAMES 3:5

A word spoken at the right time is like fruit of gold set in silver.

PROVERBS 25:11

Do not hurry to speak or be in a hurry as you think what to tell God. For God is in heaven and you are on the earth. So let your words be few.

ECCLESIASTES 5:2

A gentle answer turns away anger, but a sharp word causes anger.

PROVERBS 15:1

The mind of the one who is right with God thinks about how to answer, but the mouth of the sinful pours out sinful things.

PROVERBS 15:28

Speak with them in such a way they will want to listen to you. Do not let your talk sound foolish. Know how to give the right answer to anyone.

COLOSSIANS 4:6

The heart of the wise has power over his mouth and adds learning to his lips. Pleasing words are like honey. They are sweet to the soul and healing to the bones.

PROVERBS 16:23–24

For "If you want joy in your life and have happy days, keep your tongue from saying bad things and your lips from talking bad about others."

1 PETER 3:10

He who is always telling stories makes secrets known, but he who can be trusted keeps a thing hidden.

PROVERBS 11:13

The one who talks much will for sure sin, but he who is careful what he says is wise.

PROVERBS 10:19

A fool always loses his temper, but a wise man keeps quiet.

PROVERBS 29:11

Put out of your life these things also: anger, bad temper, bad feelings toward others, talk that hurts people, speaking against God, and dirty talk.

COLOSSIANS 3:8

O Lord, put a watch over my mouth. Keep watch over the door of my lips.

PSALM 141:3

There is one whose foolish words cut like a sword, but the tongue of the wise brings healing.

PROVERBS 12:18

We all make many mistakes. If anyone does not make a mistake with his tongue by saying the wrong things, he is a perfect man. It shows he is able to make his body do what he wants it to do.

JAMES 3:2

To give a good answer is a joy to a man, and how pleasing is a word given at the right time!

PROVERBS 15:23

There is a time to tear apart, and a time to sew together; a time to be quiet, and a time to speak.

ECCLESIASTES 3:7

COUNSEL

The true secret of giving advice is, after you have honestly given it, to be perfectly indifferent whether it is taken or not, and never persist in trying to set people right.

HANNAH WHITALL SMITH

God has given each of you a gift. Use it to help each other. This will show God's loving-favor.

1 PETER 4:10

For to us a Child will be born. To us a Son will be given. And the rule of the nations will be on His shoulders. His name will be called Wonderful, Teacher, Powerful God, Father Who Lives Forever, Prince of Peace.

ISAIAH 9:6

All your sons will be taught by the Lord, and the well-being of your children will be great.

ISAIAH 54:13

There is no joy while we are being punished. It is hard to take, but later we can see that good came from it. And it gives us the peace of being right with God.

HEBREWS 12:11

Listen to words about what you should do, and take your punishment if you need it, so that you may be wise the rest of your days.

PROVERBS 19:20

"The Holy Spirit is coming. He will lead you into all truth. He will not speak His Own words. He will speak what He hears. He will tell you of things to come."

JOHN 16:13

Give teaching to a wise man and he will be even wiser. Teach a man who is right and good, and he will grow in learning.

PROVERBS 9:9

Christian brothers, if a person is found doing some sin, you who are stronger Christians should lead that one back into the right way. Do not be proud as you do it. Watch yourself, because you may be tempted also.

GALATIANS 6:1

The way of a fool is right in his own eyes, but a wise man listens to good teaching.

PROVERBS 12:15

Oil and perfume make the heart glad, so are a man's words sweet to his friend.

PROVERBS 27:9

A nation falls where there is no wise leading, but it is safe where there are many wise men who know what to do.

PROVERBS 11:14

Plans go wrong without talking together, but they will go well when many wise men talk about what to do.

PROVERBS 15:22

The Lord punishes everyone He loves. He whips every son He receives." (Proverbs 3:11–12) Do not give up when you are punished by God. Be willing to take it, knowing that God is teaching you as a son. Is there a father who does not punish his son sometimes?

HEBREWS 12:6–7

A wise man will hear and grow in learning. A man of understanding will become able.

PROVERBS 1:5

COURAGE

You have to accept whatever comes and the only important thing is that you meet it with courage, and with the best you have to give.

ELEANOR ROOSEVELT

Only be strong and have much strength of heart. Be careful to obey all the Law which My servant Moses told you.

Do not turn from it to the right or to the left. Then all will go well with you everywhere you go.

JOSHUA 1:7

Wait for the Lord. Be strong. Let your heart be strong. Yes, wait for the Lord.

PSALM 27:14

For God did not give us a spirit of fear. He gave us a spirit of power and of love and of a good mind.

2 TIMOTHY 1:7

So we can say for sure, "The Lord is my Helper. I am not afraid of anything man can do to me." (Psalm 118:6)

HEBREWS 13:6

Live your lives as the Good News of Christ says you should. If I come to you or not, I want to hear that you are standing true as one. I want to hear that you are working together as one, preaching the Good News. Do not be afraid of those who hate you. Their hate for you proves they will be destroyed. It proves you have life from God that lasts forever.

PHILIPPIANS 1:27–28

And now, my children, live by the help of Him. Then when He comes again, we will be glad to see Him and not be ashamed.

1 JOHN 2:28

There is strong trust in the fear of the Lord, and His children will have a safe place.

PROVERBS 14:26

The sinful run away when no one is trying to catch them, but those who are right with God have as much strength of heart as a lion.

PROVERBS 28:1

Christian brothers, now we know we can go into the Holiest Place of All because the blood of Jesus was given.

HEBREWS 10:19

Be strong. Be strong in heart, all you who hope in the Lord.

PSALM 31:24

We can come to God without fear because we have put our trust in Christ.

EPHESIANS 3:12

For the Lord will be your trust. He will keep your foot from being caught.

PROVERBS 3:26

DILIGENCE

When I stand before God at the end of my life, I would hope that I would not have a single bit of talent left and could say, "I used everything you gave me."

ERMA BOMBECK

I remember my song in the night. I think with my heart. And my spirit asks questions.

PSALM 77:6

"Only be very careful to obey the Law which the Lord's servant Moses told you. Love the Lord your God. Walk in all His ways. Obey His Laws. Stay close to Him, and work for Him with all your heart and soul."

JOSHUA 22:5

Keep your heart pure for out of it are the important things of life.

PROVERBS 4:23

You are rich in everything. You have faith. You can preach. You have much learning. You have a strong desire to help. And you have love for us. Now do what you should about giving also.

2 CORINTHIANS 8:7

He who works with a lazy hand is poor, but the hand of the hard worker brings riches.

PROVERBS 10:4

The soul of the lazy person has strong desires but gets nothing, but the soul of the one who does his best gets more than he needs.

PROVERBS 13:4

Do your best to add holy living to your faith. Then add to this a better understanding. As you have a better understanding, be able to say no when you need to. Do not give up. And as you wait and do not give up, live God-like. As you live God-like, be kind to Christian brothers and love them. . . . Christian brothers, make sure you are among those He has chosen and called out for His own. As long as you do these things, you will never trip and fall.

2 PETER 1:5–7, 10

"Do not work for food that does not last. Work for food that lasts forever. The Son of Man will give you that kind of food. God the Father has shown He will do this."

JOHN 6:27

"We must keep on doing the work of Him Who sent Me while it is day. Night is coming when no man can work."

JOHN 9:4

This is what I have seen to be good and right: to eat and to drink and be happy in all the work one does under the sun during the few years of his life which God has given him. For this is his reward.

ECCLESIASTES 5:18–19

But you, Christian brothers, do not get tired of doing good.

2 THESSALONIANS 3:13

If someone has the gift of speaking words of comfort and help, he should speak. If someone has the gift of sharing what he has, he should give from a willing heart. If someone has the gift of leading other people, he should lead them. If someone has the gift of showing kindness to others, he should be happy as he does it.

ROMANS 12:8

The plans of those who do their best lead only to having all they need, but all who are in a hurry come only to want.

PROVERBS 21:5

Dear friends, since you are waiting for these things to happen, do all you can to be found by Him in peace. Be clean and free from sin.

2 PETER 3:14

Do not let yourselves get tired of doing good. If we do not give up, we will get what is coming to us at the right time.

GALATIANS 6:9

Whatever is wanted by the God of heaven, let it be done in full for the house of the God of heaven. Or else He might be angry with the nation of the king and his sons.

EZRA 7:23

So then, Christian brothers, because of all this, be strong. Do not allow anyone to change your mind. Always do your work well for the Lord. You know that whatever you do for Him will not be wasted.

1 CORINTHIANS 15:58

Much food is in the plowed land of the poor, but it is taken away because of wrong-doing.

PROVERBS 13:23

Discipline, Family

I can't think of anything parents could do to children more heartless than failing to discipline.
Janette Oke

Punish your son when he does wrong and he will give you comfort. Yes, he will give joy to your soul.
Proverbs 29:17

Do not keep from punishing the child if he needs it. If you beat him with the stick, he will not die. Beat him with the stick, and save his soul from hell.
Proverbs 23:13–14

He who does not punish his son when he needs it hates him, but he who loves him will punish him when he needs it.
Proverbs 13:24

A foolish way is held in the heart of a child, but the punishing stick will send it far from him.
Proverbs 22:15

"Now this man may have a son who has seen all the sins his father has done, but does not do the same. He does not eat at the altars on the mountains or look to the false gods of Israel. He does not sin with his neighbor's wife, or make it hard for anyone. He does not keep what another man has given him in trust for a promise. He does not steal, but he gives his bread to the hungry and clothing to those who have none. He keeps away from sin. He does not make a person pay back more than he owes him. But he walks in My Laws and obeys them. This man will not die for his father's sin. He will live for sure."

EZEKIEL 18:14–17

Punish your son if he needs it while there is hope, and do not worry about his crying.

PROVERBS 19:18

A young man makes himself known by his actions and proves if his ways are pure and right.

PROVERBS 20:11

DISCIPLINE, GOD'S

God has to punish His children from time to time, and it is the very demonstration of His love.
ELISABETH ELLIOT

O Lord, do not speak sharp words to me in Your anger, or punish me when You are angry.

PSALM 6:1

"I speak strong words to those I love and I punish them. Have a strong desire to please the Lord. Be sorry for your sins and turn from them."

REVELATION 3:19

Do you remember what God said to you when He called you His sons? "My son, listen when the Lord punishes you. Do not give up when He tells you what you must do. The Lord punishes everyone He loves. He whips every son He receives." (Proverbs 3:11–12) Do not give up when you are punished by God. Be willing to take it, knowing that God is teaching you as a son. Is there a father who does not punish his son sometimes? If you are not punished as all sons are, it means that you are not a true son of God. You are not a part of His family and He is not your Father.

HEBREWS 12:5–8

"So know in your heart that the Lord your God was punishing you just as a man punishes his son."

DEUTERONOMY 8:5

But if we would look into our own lives and see if we are guilty, then God would not have to say we are guilty. When we are guilty, we are punished by the Lord so we will not be told we are guilty with the rest of the world.

1 CORINTHIANS 11:31–32

The Lord has punished me but He has not given me over to death.

PSALM 118:18

For the word is a lamp. The teaching is a light, and strong words that punish are the way of life.

PROVERBS 6:23

Happy is the man who is punished until he gives up sin, O Lord, and whom You teach from Your Law. You give him rest from days of trouble, until a hole is dug for the sinful.

PSALM 94:12–13

The Lord punishes everyone He loves. He whips every son He receives.

PROVERBS 3:12

There is no joy while we are being punished. It is hard to take, but later we can see that good came from it. And it gives us the peace of being right with God.

HEBREWS 12:11

DUTY

Laziness may appear attractive,
but work gives satisfaction.
ANNE FRANK

The last word, after all has been heard, is: Honor God and obey His Laws. This is all that every person must do.

ECCLESIASTES 12:13

"If you think it is wrong to serve the Lord, choose today whom you will serve. Choose the gods your fathers worshiped on the other side of the river, or choose the gods of the Amorites in whose land you are living. But as for me and my family, we will serve the Lord."

JOSHUA 24:15

Now then, if you will obey My voice and keep My agreement, you will belong to Me from among all nations. For all the earth is Mine.

EXODUS 19:5

Keep His Laws which I am giving you today. Then it may go well with you and your children after you. And you may live long in the land the Lord your God is giving you for all time.

DEUTERONOMY 4:40

When the ways of a man are pleasing to the Lord, He makes even those who hate him to be at peace with him.

PROVERBS 16:7

Yet there will be no poor among you for the Lord will be sure to bring good to you in the land the Lord your God is giving you for your own. But you must listen and obey the voice of the Lord your God. Be careful to do all the Law which I am telling you today.

DEUTERONOMY 15:4–5

If you are willing and obey, you will eat the best of the land.

ISAIAH 1:19

He kept on looking to God in the days of Zechariah, who had special wisdom from God and taught him in the things of God. And as long as he looked to the Lord, God made things go well for him.

2 CHRONICLES 26:5

"And why do you call Me, 'Lord, Lord,' but do not do what I say?"

LUKE 6:46

"But I show loving-kindness to thousands of those who love Me and keep My Laws."

EXODUS 20:6

Be careful to listen to all these words I am telling you. Then it will go well with you and your children after you forever. For you will be doing what is good and right in the eyes of the Lord your God.

DEUTERONOMY 12:28

"You will be hated by all people because of Me. But he who stays true to the end will be saved."

MATTHEW 10:22

"See, I have put in front of you today life and what is good, and death and what is bad. I tell you today to love the Lord your God. Walk in His ways. Keep all His Laws and all that He has decided. Then you will live and become many. And the Lord your God will bring good to you in the land you are going in to take.

DEUTERONOMY 30:15–16

Encouragement

What men and women need is encouragement. . . .
Instead of always harping on a man's faults, tell him of his virtues. Try to pull him out of his rut of bad habits.
Eleanor H. Porter

Help each other. Speak day after day to each other while it is still today so your heart will not become hard by being fooled by sin.

Hebrews 3:13

In each city they helped the Christians to be strong and true to the faith. They told them, "We must suffer many hard things to get into the holy nation of God."

Acts 14:22

He must hold to the words of truth which he was taught. He must be able to teach the truth and show those who are against the truth that they are wrong.

Titus 1:9

Let us not stay away from church meetings. Some people are doing this all the time. Comfort each other as you see the day of His return coming near.

Hebrews 10:25

I can do all things because Christ gives me the strength.

Philippians 4:13

So then, Christian brothers, keep a strong hold on what we have taught you by what we have said and by what we have written. Our Lord Jesus Christ and God our Father loves us. Through His loving-favor He gives us comfort and hope that lasts forever. May He give your hearts comfort and strength to say and do every good thing.

2 THESSALONIANS 2:15–17

He gives strength to the weak. And He gives power to him who has little strength.

ISAIAH 40:29

"When they take you to the places of worship and to the courts and to the leaders of the country, do not be worried about what you should say or how to say it. The Holy Spirit will tell you what you should say at that time."

LUKE 12:11–12

So comfort each other and make each other strong as you are already doing.

1 THESSALONIANS 5:11

But if we are in trouble, it is for your good. And it is so you will be saved from the punishment of sin. If God comforts us, it is for your good also. You too will be given strength not to give up when you have the same kind of trouble we have.

2 CORINTHIANS 1:6

Help each other in troubles and problems. This is the kind of law Christ asks us to obey.

GALATIANS 6:2

You know, and so does God, how pure and right and without blame we were among you who believe. As a father helps his children, you know how we wanted to help you and give you comfort. We told you with strong words that you should live to please God. He is the One Who chose you to come into His holy nation and to share His shining-greatness. We always thank God that when you heard the Word of God from us, you believed it. You did not receive it as from men, but you received it as the Word of God. That is what it is. It is at work in the lives of you who believe.

1 THESSALONIANS 2:10–13

Do not always be thinking about your own plans only. Be happy to know what other people are doing.

PHILIPPIANS 2:4

All the Holy Writings are God-given and are made alive by Him. Man is helped when he is taught God's Word. It shows what is wrong. It changes the way of a man's life. It shows him how to be right with God.

2 TIMOTHY 3:16

My Christian brothers, if any of you should be led away from the truth, let someone turn him back again. That person should know that if he turns a sinner from the wrong way, he will save the sinner's soul from death and many sins will be forgiven.

JAMES 5:19–20

Eternity

Redeemed, how I love to proclaim it!
His child, and forever, I am.
Fanny Crosby

"There are many rooms in My Father's house. If it were not so, I would have told you. I am going away to make a place for you. After I go and make a place for you, I will come back and take you with Me. Then you may be where I am."

John 14:2–3

There is a crown which comes from being right with God. The Lord, the One Who will judge, will give it to me on that great day when He comes again. I will not be the only one to receive a crown. All those who love to think of His coming and are looking for Him will receive one also.

2 Timothy 4:8

Then I saw a new heaven and a new earth. The first heaven and the first earth had passed away. There was no more sea. I saw the Holy City, the new Jerusalem. It was coming down out of heaven from God. It was made ready like a bride is made ready for her husband.

Revelation 21:1–2

He said to them, "You will suffer as I will suffer. But the places at My right side and at My left side are not Mine to give. Whoever My Father says will have those places."

Matthew 20:23

"I give them life that lasts forever. They will never be punished. No one is able to take them out of My hand."

JOHN 10:28

"Anyone who loves his life will lose it. Anyone who hates his life in this world will keep it forever."

JOHN 12:25

You get what is coming to you when you sin. It is death! But God's free gift is life that lasts forever. It is given to us by our Lord Jesus Christ.

ROMANS 6:23

Our body is like a house we live in here on earth. When it is destroyed, we know that God has another body for us in heaven. The new one will not be made by human hands as a house is made. This body will last forever.

2 CORINTHIANS 5:1

For sure, I am telling you a secret. We will not all die, but we will all be changed. In a very short time, no longer than it takes for the eye to close and open, the Christians who have died will be raised. It will happen when the last horn sounds. The dead will be raised never to die again. Then the rest of us who are alive will be changed. Our human bodies made from dust must be changed into a body that cannot be destroyed. Our human bodies that can die must be changed into bodies that will never die. When this that can be destroyed has been changed into that which cannot be destroyed, and when this that does die has been changed into that which cannot die, then it will happen as the Holy Writings said it would happen. They said, "Death has no more power over life." (Isaiah 25:8)

1 CORINTHIANS 15:51–54

We are looking for what God has promised, which are new heavens and a new earth. Only what is right and good will be there.

2 PETER 3:13

If a man does things to please his sinful old self, his soul will be lost. If a man does things to please the Holy Spirit, he will have life that lasts forever.

GALATIANS 6:8

When the Head Shepherd comes again, you will get the crown of shining-greatness that will not come to an end.

1 PETER 5:4

Many of those who sleep in the dust of the earth will wake up. Some will have life that lasts forever, but others will have shame and will suffer much forever.

DANIEL 12:2

Jesus said to her, "I am the One Who raises the dead and gives them life. Anyone who puts his trust in Me will live again, even if he dies. Anyone who lives and has put his trust in Me will never die. Do you believe this?"

JOHN 11:25–26

"You do read the Holy Writings. You think you have life that lasts forever just because you read them. They do tell of Me."

JOHN 5:39

God. . .will give to every man what he should get for the things he has done. Those who keep on doing good and are looking for His greatness and honor will receive life that lasts forever.

ROMANS 2:5–7

"Do not work for food that does not last. Work for food that lasts forever. The Son of Man will give you that kind of food. God the Father has shown He will do this."

JOHN 6:27

The Holy Spirit raised Jesus from the dead. If the same Holy Spirit lives in you, He will give life to your bodies in the same way.

ROMANS 8:11

There will be no night there. There will be no need for a light or for the sun. Because the Lord God will be their light. They will be leaders forever.

REVELATION 22:5

"For sure, I tell you, anyone who hears My Word and puts his trust in Him Who sent Me has life that lasts forever. He will not be guilty. He has already passed from death into life."

JOHN 5:24

The world and all its desires will pass away. But the man who obeys God and does what He wants done will live forever.

1 JOHN 2:17

Let us thank the God and Father of our Lord Jesus Christ. It was through His loving-kindness that we were born again to a new life and have a hope that never dies. This hope is ours because Jesus was raised from the dead. We will receive the great things that we have been promised. They are being kept safe in heaven for us. They are pure and will not pass away. They will never be lost. You are being kept by the power of God because you put your trust in Him and you will be saved from the punishment of sin at the end of the world.

1 PETER 1:3–5

For this reason they are before the throne of God. They help Him day and night in the house of God. And He Who sits on the throne will care for them as He is among them. They will never be hungry or thirsty again. The sun or any burning heat will not shine down on them. For the Lamb Who is in the center of the throne will be their Shepherd. He will lead them to wells of the water of life. God will take away all tears from their eyes."

REVELATION 7:15–17

FAITH

Faith sees the invisible, believes the unbelievable, and receives the impossible.

CORRIE TEN BOOM

You must have faith as you ask Him. You must not doubt. Anyone who doubts is like a wave which is pushed around by the sea.

JAMES 1:6

The Lord said, "If your faith was as a mustard seed, you could say to this tree, 'Be pulled out of the ground and planted in the sea,' and it would obey you."

LUKE 17:6

You have never seen Him but you love Him. You cannot see Him now but you are putting your trust in Him. And you have joy so great that words cannot tell about it.

1 PETER 1:8

Jesus heard this. He said to the leader of the Jewish place of worship, "Do not be afraid, just believe."

MARK 5:36

He said to the woman, "Your faith has saved you from the punishment of sin. Go in peace."

LUKE 7:50

You are now children of God because you have put your trust in Christ Jesus.

GALATIANS 3:26

He gave the right and the power to become children of God to those who received Him. He gave this to those who put their trust in His name.

JOHN 1:12

"He who puts his trust in Me and is baptized will be saved from the punishment of sin. But he who does not put his trust in Me is guilty and will be punished forever."

MARK 16:16

Now faith is being sure we will get what we hope for. It is being sure of what we cannot see.

HEBREWS 11:1

I pray that Christ may live in your hearts by faith. I pray that you will be filled with love. I pray that you will be able to understand how wide and how long and how high and how deep His love is. I pray that you will know the love of Christ. His love goes beyond anything we can understand. I pray that you will be filled with God Himself.

EPHESIANS 3:17–19

Jesus said to him, "Why do you ask Me that? The one who has faith can do all things."

MARK 9:23

"The early preachers wrote, 'They will all be taught of God.' (Isaiah 54:13) Everyone who listens to the Father and learns from Him comes to Me."

JOHN 6:45

In this way, you do not have faith in Christ because of the wisdom of men. You have faith in Christ because of the power of God.

1 CORINTHIANS 2:5

If you say with your mouth that Jesus is Lord, and believe in your heart that God raised Him from the dead, you will be saved from the punishment of sin.

ROMANS 10:9

Jesus said to them, "Have faith in God. For sure, I tell you, a person may say to this mountain, 'Move from here into the sea.' And if he does not doubt, but believes that what he says will be done, it will happen."

MARK 11:22–23

For by His loving-favor you have been saved from the punishment of sin through faith. It is not by anything you have done. It is a gift of God.

EPHESIANS 2:8

Jesus said to him, "Thomas, because you have seen Me, you believe. Those are happy who have never seen Me and yet believe!"

JOHN 20:29

A man cannot please God unless he has faith. Anyone who comes to God must believe that He is. That one must also know that God gives what is promised to the one who keeps on looking for Him.

HEBREWS 11:6

Our life is lived by faith. We do not live by what we see in front of us.

2 CORINTHIANS 5:7

Jesus said to them, "This is the work of God, that you put your trust in the One He has sent."

JOHN 6:29

And so let us come near to God with a true heart full of faith. Our hearts must be made clean from guilty feelings and our bodies washed with pure water.

HEBREWS 10:22

The person who puts his trust in God's Son knows in his own heart that Jesus is the Son of God. The person who does not have his trust in God's Son makes God a liar. It is because he has not believed the word God spoke about His Son.

1 JOHN 5:10

As you have put your trust in Christ Jesus the Lord to save you from the punishment of sin, now let Him lead you in every step. Have your roots planted deep in Christ. Grow in Him. Get your strength from Him. Let Him make you strong in the faith as you have been taught. Your life should be full of thanks to Him.

COLOSSIANS 2:6–7

"See! I stand at the door and knock. If anyone hears My voice and opens the door, I will come in to him and we will eat together."

REVELATION 3:20

I have been put up on the cross to die with Christ. I no longer live. Christ lives in me. The life I now live in this body, I live by putting my trust in the Son of God. He was the One Who loved me and gave Himself for me.

GALATIANS 2:20

FAITHFULNESS OF GOD

God tries our faith so that
we may try His faithfulness.
UNKNOWN

We know that God makes all things work together for the good of those who love Him and are chosen to be a part of His plan.

ROMANS 8:28

O Lord, the heavens will praise Your great works and how faithful You are in the meeting of the holy ones.

PSALM 89:5

A faithful man will have many good things, but he who hurries to be rich will be punished for it.

PROVERBS 28:20

This truth also gives hope of life that lasts forever. God promised this before the world began. He cannot lie.

TITUS 1:2

"Who is the faithful and wise servant whom his owner has made boss over the other servants? He is to have food ready for them at the right time. That servant is happy who is doing what his owner wants him to do when he comes back. For sure, I tell you, he will make him boss over all that he has."

MATTHEW 24:45–47

So the Lord God says, "See, I lay in Jerusalem a Stone of great worth to build upon, a tested Stone. Anyone who puts his trust in Him will not be afraid of what will happen.

ISAIAH 28:16

If we have no faith, He will still be faithful for He cannot go against what He is.

2 TIMOTHY 2:13

The Lord is not slow about keeping His promise as some people think. He is waiting for you. The Lord does not want any person to be punished forever. He wants all people to be sorry for their sins and turn from them.

2 PETER 3:9

For the Lord your God is a God of loving-pity. He will not leave you or destroy you or forget the agreement He promised to your fathers.

DEUTERONOMY 4:31

Let us hold on to the hope we say we have and not be changed. We can trust God that He will do what He promised.

HEBREWS 10:23

"Do not be afraid of what you will suffer. Listen! The devil will throw some of you into prison to test you. You will be in trouble for ten days. Be faithful even to death. Then I will give you the crown of life."

REVELATION 2:10

God is not a man, that He should lie. He is not a son of man, that He should be sorry for what He has said. Has He said, and will He not do it? Has He spoken, and will He not keep His Word?

NUMBERS 23:19

"Thanks be to the Lord. He has given rest to His people Israel. He has done all that He promised. Every word has come true of all His good promise, which He promised through His servant Moses."

1 KINGS 8:56

Love the Lord, all you who belong to Him! The Lord keeps the faithful safe. But He gives the proud their pay in full.

PSALM 31:23

Know then that the Lord your God is God, the faithful God. He keeps His promise and shows His loving-kindness to those who love Him and keep His Laws, even to a thousand family groups in the future.

DEUTERONOMY 7:9

FEARING GOD

Reverence for the Lord is the beginning of wisdom.
ELISABETH ELLIOT

"Do not be afraid of them who kill the body. They are not able to kill the soul. But fear Him Who is able to destroy both soul and body in hell."

MATTHEW 10:28

"Also, you should choose from the people able men who fear God, men of truth who hate to get things by doing wrong. Have these men rule over the people, as leaders of thousands, of hundreds, of fifties and of tens."

EXODUS 18:21

The fear of the Lord is the beginning of much learning. Fools hate wisdom and teaching.

PROVERBS 1:7

He said with a loud voice, "Honor God with love and fear. The time has come for Him to judge all men. Worship Him Who made heaven and earth and the sea and the places where water comes out of the earth."

REVELATION 14:7

If only they had such a heart in them that they would fear Me and live by all My Laws always! Then it would go well with them and with their children forever.

DEUTERONOMY 5:29

The angel of the Lord stays close around those who fear Him, and He takes them out of trouble.

PSALM 34:7

You believe there is one God. That is good! But even the demons believe that, and because they do, they shake.

JAMES 2:19

"Only fear the Lord and be faithful to worship Him with all your heart. Think of the great things He has done for you."

1 SAMUEL 12:24

A wise man fears God and turns away from what is sinful, but a fool is full of pride and is not careful.

PROVERBS 14:16

Since we have received a holy nation that cannot be moved, let us be thankful. Let us please God and worship Him with honor and fear. For our God is a fire that destroys everything.

HEBREWS 12:28–29

My Christian friends, you have obeyed me when I was with you. You have obeyed even more when I have been away. You must keep on working to show you have been saved from the punishment of sin. Be afraid that you may not please God.

PHILIPPIANS 2:12

Since we have these great promises, dear friends, let us turn away from every sin of the body or of the spirit. Let us honor God with love and fear by giving ourselves to Him in every way.

2 CORINTHIANS 7:1

He will fill the desire of those who fear Him. He will also hear their cry and will save them.

PSALM 145:19

The fear of the Lord is to hate what is sinful. I hate pride, self-love, the way of sin, and lies.

PROVERBS 8:13

The last word, after all has been heard, is: Honor God and obey His Laws. This is all that every person must do.

ECCLESIASTES 12:13

The secret of the Lord is for those who fear Him. And He will make them know His agreement.

PSALM 25:14

" 'Do you not fear Me?' says the Lord. 'Do you not shake in fear before Me? For I have placed the sand to be on one side of the sea, a lasting wall that it cannot cross. Even if there are waves, they cannot pass. Even if they make much noise, they cannot cross over it.' "

JEREMIAH 5:22

Serve the Lord with fear, and be full of joy as you shake in fear.

PSALM 2:11

Then those who feared the Lord spoke often to one another, and the Lord listened to them. And the names of those who worshiped the Lord and honored Him were written down before Him in a Book to be remembered.

MALACHI 3:16

FORGIVENESS

If the wounds of millions are to be healed, what other way is there except through forgiveness?
CATHERINE MARSHALL

You must be kind to each other. Think of the other person. Forgive other people just as God forgave you because of Christ's death on the cross.

EPHESIANS 4:32

Try to understand other people. Forgive each other. If you have something against someone, forgive him. That is the way the Lord forgave you.

COLOSSIANS 3:13

When someone does something bad to you, do not do the same thing to him. When someone talks about you, do not talk about him. Instead, pray that good will come to him. You were called to do this so you might receive good things from God.

1 PETER 3:9

"If you forgive people their sins, your Father in heaven will forgive your sins also. If you do not forgive people their sins, your Father will not forgive your sins."

MATTHEW 6:14–15

Then Peter came to Jesus and said, "Lord, how many times may my brother sin against me and I forgive him, up to seven times?" Jesus said to him, "I tell you, not seven times but seventy times seven!"

MATTHEW 18:21–22

"Watch yourselves! If your brother sins, speak sharp words to him. If he is sorry and turns from his sin, forgive him. What if he sins against you seven times in one day? If he comes to you and says he is sorry and turns from his sin, forgive him."

LUKE 17:3–4

"When you stand to pray, if you have anything against anyone, forgive him. Then your Father in heaven will forgive your sins also. *If you do not forgive them their sins, your Father in heaven will not forgive your sins."

MARK 11:25–26

"Forgive us our sins, as we forgive those who sin against us. Do not let us be tempted."

LUKE 11:4

A man's understanding makes him slow to anger. It is to his honor to forgive and forget a wrong done to him.

PROVERBS 19:11

"But I tell you, do not fight with the man who wants to fight. Whoever hits you on the right side of the face, turn so he can hit the other side also. If any person takes you to court to get your shirt, give him your coat also. Whoever makes you walk a short way, go with him twice as far."

MATTHEW 5:39–41

"Forgive us our sins as we forgive those who sin against us."

MATTHEW 6:12

"If My people who are called by My name put away their pride and pray, and look for My face, and turn from their sinful ways, then I will hear from heaven. I will forgive their sin, and will heal their land."

2 CHRONICLES 7:14

For You are good and ready to forgive, O Lord. You are rich in loving-kindness to all who call to You.

PSALM 86:5

"Do not say what is wrong in other people's lives. Then other people will not say what is wrong in your life. Do not say someone is guilty. Then other people will not say you are guilty. Forgive other people and other people will forgive you."

LUKE 6:37

He turned to the woman and said to Simon, "Do you see this woman? I came into your house and you gave Me no water to wash My feet. She washed My feet with her tears and dried them with the hairs of her head. You gave me no kiss, but this woman has kissed my feet from the time I came in. You did not put even oil on My head but this woman has put special perfume on My feet. I tell you, her many sins are forgiven because she loves much. But the one who has been forgiven little, loves little." Then He said to the woman, "Your sins are forgiven."

LUKE 7:44–48

FRIENDSHIP

My friends are my estate.
EMILY DICKINSON

Iron is made sharp with iron, and one man is made sharp by a friend.

PROVERBS 27:17

A friend loves at all times. A brother is born to share troubles.

PROVERBS 17:17

A man who has friends must be a friend, but there is a friend who stays nearer than a brother.

PROVERBS 18:24

Jesus said to them, "If one of you has a friend and goes to him in the night and says, 'Friend, give me three loaves of bread, for a friend of mine is on a trip and has stopped at my house. I have no food to give him.' The man inside the house will say, 'Do not trouble me. The door is shut. My children and I are in bed. I cannot get up and give you bread.' I say to you, he may not get up and give him bread because he is a friend. Yet, if he keeps on asking, he will get up and give him as much as he needs."

LUKE 11:5–8

"Kindness from a friend should be shown to a man without hope, or he might turn away from the fear of the All-powerful."

JOB 6:14

The pains given by a friend are faithful, but the kisses of one who hates you are false.

PROVERBS 27:6

Do you not know that to love the sinful things of the world and to be a friend to them is to be against God? Yes, I say it again, if you are a friend of the world, you are against God.

JAMES 4:4

GENEROSITY

It's not how much we give but how much love we put into giving.
MOTHER TERESA

He has given much to the poor. His right-standing with God lasts forever. His horn will be lifted high in honor.

PSALM 112:9

Tell those who are rich in this world not to be proud and not to trust in their money. Money cannot be trusted. They should put their trust in God. He gives us all we need for our happiness. Tell them to do good and be rich in good works. They should give much to those in need and be ready to share.

1 TIMOTHY 6:17–18

"When you have a supper, ask poor people. Ask those who cannot walk and those who are blind. You will be happy if you do this. They cannot pay you back. You will get your pay when the people who are right with God are raised from the dead."

LUKE 14:13–14

Do not keep good from those who should have it, when it is in your power to do it. Do not say to your neighbor, "Go, and return tomorrow, and I will give it," when you have it with you.

PROVERBS 3:27–28

He answered them, "If you have two coats, give one to him who has none. If you have food, you must share some."

LUKE 3:11

"When you give to the poor, do not be as those who pretend to be someone they are not. They blow a horn in the places of worship and in the streets so people may respect them. For sure, I tell you, they have all the reward they are going to get. When you give, do not let your left hand know what your right hand gives. Your giving should be in secret. Then your Father Who sees in secret will reward you."

MATTHEW 6:2–4

He who hates his neighbor sins, but happy is he who shows loving-favor to the poor.

PROVERBS 14:21

"If your brother becomes poor and is not able to pay you what he owes, then you should help him as you would help a stranger or visitor. So he may live with you."

LEVITICUS 25:35

If you have any women whose husbands have died in your family, you must care for them. The church should not have to help them. The church can help women whose husbands have died who are all alone in this world and have no one else to help them.

1 TIMOTHY 5:16

He saw a poor woman whose husband had died. She put in two very small pieces of money. He said, "I tell you the truth, this poor woman has put in more than all of them. For they have put in a little of the money they had no need for. She is very poor and has put in all she had. She has put in what she needed for her own living."

LUKE 21:2–4

The poor will always be in the land. So I tell you to be free in giving to your brother, to those in need, and to the poor in your land.

DEUTERONOMY 15:11

What if a Christian does not have clothes or food? And one of you says to him, "Goodbye, keep yourself warm and eat well." But if you do not give him what he needs, how does that help him?

JAMES 2:15–16

Happy is the man who cares for the poor. The Lord will save him in times of trouble. The Lord will keep him alive and safe. And he will be happy upon the earth. You will not give him over to the desire of those who hate him.

PSALM 41:1–2

Each man should give as he has decided in his heart. He should not give, wishing he could keep it. Or he should not give if he feels he has to give. God loves a man who gives because he wants to give.

2 CORINTHIANS 9:7

"Then the King will say to those on His right side, 'Come, you who have been called by My Father. Come into the holy nation that has been made ready for you before the world was made. For I was hungry and you gave Me food to eat. I was thirsty and you gave Me water to drink. I was a stranger and you gave Me a room. I had no clothes and you gave Me clothes to wear. I was sick and you cared for Me. I was in prison and you came to see Me.' Then those that are right with God will say, 'Lord, when did we see You hungry and feed You? When did we see You thirsty and give You a drink? When did we see You a stranger and give You a room? When did we see You had no clothes and we gave You clothes? And when did we see You sick or in prison and we came to You?' Then the King will say, 'For sure, I tell you, because you did it to one of the least of My brothers, you have done it to Me.' "

MATTHEW 25:34–40

Is it not a time to share your food with the hungry, and bring the poor man into your house who has no home of his own? Is it not a time to give clothes to the person you see who has no clothes, and a time not to hide yourself from your own family? Then your light will break out like the early morning, and you will soon be healed. Your right and good works will go before you. And the shining-greatness of the Lord will keep watch behind you.

Isaiah 58:7–8

"For sure, I tell you, whoever gives you a cup of water to drink in My name because you belong to Christ will not lose his reward from God."

Mark 9:41

Every man should give as he is able, as the Lord your God has given to you.

Deuteronomy 16:17

"Give, and it will be given to you. You will have more than enough. It can be pushed down and shaken together and it will still run over as it is given to you. The way you give to others is the way you will receive in return."

Luke 6:38

You know of the loving-favor shown by our Lord Jesus Christ. He was rich, but He became poor for your good. In that way, because He became poor, you might become rich.

2 Corinthians 8:9

He who shows kindness to a poor man gives to the Lord and He will pay him in return for his good act.

Proverbs 19:17

"In every way I showed you that by working hard like this we can help those who are weak. We must remember what the Lord Jesus said, 'We are more happy when we give than when we receive.' "

ACTS 20:35

Sell what you have and give the money to poor people. Have money-bags for yourselves that will never wear out. These money-bags are riches in heaven that will always be there. No robber can take them and no bugs can eat them there. Your heart will be wherever your riches are.

LUKE 12:33–34

Most of all, have a true love for each other. Love covers many sins. Be happy to have people stay for the night and eat with you. God has given each of you a gift. Use it to help each other. This will show God's loving-favor.

1 PETER 4:8–10

GENTLENESS

Take my heart and make it your dwelling place so that everyone I touch will be touched also by you!
ALICE JOYCE DAVIDSON

"Follow My teachings and learn from Me. I am gentle and do not have pride. You will have rest for your souls."

MATTHEW 11:29

I, Paul, ask you this myself. I do it through Christ Who is so gentle and kind. Some people say that I am gentle and quiet when I am with you, but that I have no fear and that my language is strong when I am away from you.

2 CORINTHIANS 10:1

Teach your people to obey the leaders of their country. They should be ready to do any good work. They must not speak bad of anyone, and they must not argue. They should be gentle and kind to all people.

TITUS 3:1–2

He will feed His flock like a shepherd. He will gather the lambs in His arms and carry them close to His heart. He will be gentle in leading those that are with young.

ISAIAH 40:11

But the fruit that comes from having the Holy Spirit in our lives is: love, joy, peace, not giving up, being kind, being good, having faith. . . .

GALATIANS 5:22

A servant owned by God must not make trouble. He must be kind to everyone. He must be able to teach. He must be willing to suffer when hurt for doing good. Be gentle when you try to teach those who are against what you say. God may change their hearts so they will turn to the truth. Then they will know they had been held in a trap by the devil to do what he wanted them to do. But now they are able to get out of it.

2 TIMOTHY 2:24–26

Those who suffer will eat and have enough. Those who look for the Lord will praise Him. May your heart live forever!

PSALM 22:26

But the wisdom that comes from heaven is first of all pure. Then it gives peace. It is gentle and willing to obey. It is full of loving-kindness and of doing good. It has no doubts and does not pretend to be something it is not.

JAMES 3:17

The Lord lifts up those who are suffering, and He brings the sinful down to the ground.

PSALM 147:6

Instead, we were gentle when we came to you. We were like a mother caring for her children. We had such a strong desire to help you that we were happy to give you the Good News. Because we loved you so much, we were ready to give you our own lives also.

1 THESSALONIANS 2:7–8

GOD'S LOVE

Love has its source in God, for love is the very essence of His being.

KAY ARTHUR

See what great love the Father has for us that He would call us His children. And that is what we are. For this reason the people of the world do not know who we are because they did not know Him.

1 John 3:1

God has shown His love to us by sending His only Son into the world. God did this so we might have life through Christ.

1 John 4:9

"I will bring My people back to Me. I will not hold back My love from them, for I am no longer angry with them."

Hosea 14:4

The Holy Writings say, "No eye has ever seen or no ear has ever heard or no mind has ever thought of the wonderful things God has made ready for those who love Him." (Isaiah 64:4; 65:17)

1 Corinthians 2:9

For I know that nothing can keep us from the love of God. Death cannot! Life cannot! Angels cannot! Leaders cannot! Any other power cannot! Hard things now or in the future cannot! The world above or the world below cannot! Any other living thing cannot keep us away from the love of God which is ours through Christ Jesus our Lord.

Romans 8:38–39

Hope never makes us ashamed because the love of God has come into our hearts through the Holy Spirit Who was given to us.

Romans 5:5

We have come to know and believe the love God has for us. God is love. If you live in love, you live by the help of God and God lives in you.

1 JOHN 4:16

This is love! It is not that we loved God but that He loved us. For God sent His Son to pay for our sins with His own blood.

1 JOHN 4:10

The Lord takes care of all who love Him.

PSALM 145:20

"For God so loved the world that He gave His only Son. Whoever puts his trust in God's Son will not be lost but will have life that lasts forever."

JOHN 3:16

But God showed His love to us. While we were still sinners, Christ died for us.

ROMANS 5:8

"The Father loves you. He loves you because you love Me and believe that I came from the Father."

JOHN 16:27

God's Provision

Lift up your eyes. Your heavenly Father waits to bless you in inconceivable ways to make your life what you never dreamed it could be.
Annie Ortlund

The young lions suffer want and hunger. But they who look for the Lord will not be without any good thing.
Psalm 34:10

And my God will give you everything you need because of His great riches in Christ Jesus.
Philippians 4:19

He gives food to those who fear Him. He will remember His agreement forever.
Psalm 111:5

"I tell you this: Do not worry about your life. Do not worry about what you are going to eat and drink. Do not worry about what you are going to wear. Is not life more important than food? Is not the body more important than clothes? Look at the birds in the sky. They do not plant seeds. They do not gather grain. They do not put grain into a building to keep. Yet your Father in heaven feeds them! Are you not more important than the birds? Which of you can make himself a little taller by worrying? Why should you worry about clothes? Think how the flowers grow. They do not work or make cloth. But I tell you that Solomon in all his greatness was not dressed as well as one of these flowers. God clothes the grass of the field. It lives today and is burned in the stove tomorrow. How much more will He give you clothes? You have so little faith! Do not worry. Do not keep saying, 'What will we eat?' or, 'What will we drink?' or, 'What will we wear?' The people who do not know God are looking for all these things. Your Father in heaven knows you need all these things. First of all, look for the holy nation of God. Be right with Him. All these other things will be given to you also."

MATTHEW 6:25–33

Tell those who are rich in this world not to be proud and not to trust in their money. Money cannot be trusted. They should put their trust in God. He gives us all we need for our happiness.

1 TIMOTHY 6:17

GRATITUDE

Simple gratitude helps us experience God at work in every moment of every day.
HARRIET CROSBY

I will give thanks to the Lord with all my heart. I will tell of all the great things You have done. I will be glad and full of joy because of You. I will sing praise to Your name, O Most High.

PSALM 9:1–2

I will speak with the voice of thanks, and tell of all Your great works.

PSALM 26:7

"Thanks be to the Lord. He has given rest to His people Israel. He has done all that He promised. Every word has come true of all His good promise, which He promised through His servant Moses."

1 KINGS 8:56

The man who worships on a special day does it to honor the Lord. The man who eats meat does it to honor the Lord. He gives thanks to God for what he eats. The other man does not eat meat. In this way, he honors the Lord. He gives thanks to God also.

ROMANS 14:6

Always give thanks for all things to God the Father in the name of our Lord Jesus Christ.

EPHESIANS 5:20

You have turned my crying into dancing. You have taken off my clothes made from hair, and dressed me with joy. So my soul may sing praise to You, and not be quiet. O Lord my God, I will give thanks to You forever.

PSALM 30:11–12

Day after day they went to the house of God together. In their houses they ate their food together. Their hearts were happy. They gave thanks to God and all the people respected them. The Lord added to the group each day those who were being saved from the punishment of sin.

ACTS 2:46–47

O Lord my God, many are the great works You have done, and Your thoughts toward us. No one can compare with You! If I were to speak and tell of them, there would be too many to number.

PSALM 40:5

I will tell of the loving-kindness of the Lord, and praise Him for all He has done. I will tell of all the Lord has given us, the great goodness He has shown to the family of Israel and given to them because of His loving-pity and His great loving-kindness.

ISAIAH 63:7

Honor and thanks be to the Lord, Who carries our heavy loads day by day. He is the God Who saves us.

PSALM 68:19

I give thanks and praise to You, O God of my fathers. For You have given me wisdom and power. Even now You have made known what we asked of You. You have made the king's dream known to us.

DANIEL 2:23

In everything give thanks. This is what God wants you to do because of Christ Jesus.

1 THESSALONIANS 5:18

It is good to give thanks to the Lord, and sing praises to Your name, O Most High. It is good to tell of Your loving-kindness in the morning, and of how faithful You are at night.

PSALM 92:1–2

Then He took the seven loaves of bread and the fish and gave thanks. He broke them and gave them to His followers. The followers gave them to the people.

MATTHEW 15:36

Give thanks to the Lord, for He is good, for His loving-kindness lasts forever.

PSALM 136:1

HONESTY

Do not do what you would undo if caught.
LEAH ARENDT

Christian brothers, keep your minds thinking about whatever is true, whatever is respected, whatever is right, whatever is pure, whatever can be loved, and whatever is well thought of. If there is anything good and worth giving thanks for, think about these things.

PHILIPPIANS 4:8

You who are servants who are owned by someone, obey your owners. Work hard for them all the time, not just when they are watching you. Work for them as you would for the Lord because you honor God.

COLOSSIANS 3:22

Do not steal. Be honest in what you do. Do not lie to one another.

LEVITICUS 19:11

Night is almost gone. Day is almost here. We must stop doing the sinful things that are done in the dark. We must put on all the things God gives us to fight with for the day. We must act all the time as if it were day. Keep away from wild parties and do not be drunk. Keep yourself free from sex sins and bad actions. Do not fight or be jealous.

ROMANS 13:12–13

Pray for us. Our hearts tell us we are right. We want to do the right thing always.

HEBREWS 13:18

Do your best to live a quiet life. Learn to do your own work well. We told you about this before. By doing this, you will be respected by those who are not Christians. Then you will not be in need and others will not have to help you.

1 THESSALONIANS 4:11–12

Live in peace with each other. Do not act or think with pride. Be happy to be with poor people. Keep yourself from thinking you are so wise. When someone does something bad to you, do not pay him back with something bad. Try to do what all men know is right and good.

ROMANS 12:16–17

Do not lie to each other. You have put out of your life your old ways. You have now become a new person and are always learning more about Christ. You are being made more like Christ. He is the One Who made you.

COLOSSIANS 3:9–10

We want to do the right thing. We want God and men to know we are honest.

2 CORINTHIANS 8:21

He gives money to be used without being paid for its use. And he does not take money to hurt those who are not guilty. He who does these things will never be shaken.

PSALM 15:5

I always try to live so my own heart tells me I am not guilty before God or man.

ACTS 24:16

"You know the Laws, 'Do not be guilty of sex sins in marriage. Do not kill another person. Do not take things from people in wrong ways. Do not steal. Do not lie. Respect your father and mother.' "

MARK 10:19

He who walks with God, and whose words are good and honest, he who will not take money received from wrong-doing, and will not receive money given in secret for wrong-doing, he who stops his ears from hearing about killing, and shuts his eyes from looking at what is sinful, he will have a place on high. His safe place will be a rock that cannot be taken over. He will be given food and will have water for sure.

ISAIAH 33:15–16

"Do for other people whatever you would like to have them do for you. This is what the Jewish Law and the early preachers said."

MATTHEW 7:12

"Do for other people what you would like to have them do for you."

LUKE 6:31

Tax-gatherers came to be baptized also. They asked him, "Teacher, what are we to do?" He said to them, "Do not take more money from people than you should."

LUKE 3:12–13

He who has clean hands and a pure heart. He who has not lifted up his soul to what is not true, and has not made false promises.

PSALM 24:4

Receive us into your hearts. We have done no wrong to anyone. We have not led anyone in the wrong way. We have not used anyone for our good.

2 CORINTHIANS 7:2

"I hold on to what is right and good and will not let it go. My heart does not put me to shame for any of my days."

JOB 27:6

HONOR

Let our actions make us worthy of the blessing we have received and [pray] that God will continue to bless us!

DIANE ALBERS

Honor the Lord with your riches, and with the first of all you grow.

PROVERBS 3:9

Children, as Christians, obey your parents. This is the right thing to do. Respect your father and mother. This is the first Law given that had a promise. The promise is this: If you respect your father and mother, you will live a long time and your life will be full of many good things.

EPHESIANS 6:1–3

"Honor your father and your mother, so your life may be long in the land the Lord your God gives you."

EXODUS 20:12

She is worth more than stones of great worth. Nothing you can wish for compares with her. Long life is in her right hand. Riches and honor are in her left hand.

PROVERBS 3:15–16

"If you keep from doing what pleases you on the Day of Rest, on My holy day and call the Day of Rest a happy time, and respect the holy day of the Lord, and if you honor it by turning from your own ways, and from following your own desire and by not talking in a foolish way, then you will have joy in the Lord. I will cause you to ride on the high places of the earth. And I will feed you with the best from the land given to your father Jacob. The mouth of the Lord has spoken."

ISAIAH 58:13–14

Hope

Optimism is the faith that leads to achievement.
Nothing can be done without hope and confidence.
Helen Keller

Dear friends, we are God's children now. But it has not yet been shown to us what we are going to be. We know that when He comes again, we will be like Him because we will see Him as He is. The person who is looking for this to happen will keep himself pure because Christ is pure.
1 John 3:2–3

We are glad for our troubles also. We know that troubles help us learn not to give up. When we have learned not to give up, it shows we have stood the test. When we have stood the test, it gives us hope. Hope never makes us ashamed because the love of God has come into our hearts through the Holy Spirit Who was given to us.
Romans 5:3–5

The hope of those who are right with God is joy, but the hope of the sinful comes to nothing.
Proverbs 10:28

Let us thank the God and Father of our Lord Jesus Christ. It was through His loving-kindness that we were born again to a new life and have a hope that never dies. This hope is ours because Jesus was raised from the dead.
1 Peter 1:3

Good will come to the man who trusts in the Lord, and whose hope is in the Lord.

JEREMIAH 17:7

Christian brothers, we want you to know for sure about those who have died. You have no reason to have sorrow as those who have no hope. We believe that Jesus died and then came to life again. Because we believe this, we know that God will bring to life again all those who belong to Jesus.

1 THESSALONIANS 4:13–14

You are my hiding place and my battle-covering. I put my hope in Your Word.

PSALM 119:114

"The Lord is my share," says my soul, "so I have hope in Him." The Lord is good to those who wait for Him, to the one who looks for Him. It is good that one should be quiet and wait for the saving power of the Lord.

LAMENTATIONS 3:24–26

Because we are men of the day, let us keep our minds awake. Let us cover our chests with faith and love. Let us cover our heads with the hope of being saved.

1 THESSALONIANS 5:8

My soul becomes weak with desire for Your saving power, but I have put my hope in Your Word.

PSALM 119:81

Your heart should be holy and set apart for the Lord God. Always be ready to tell everyone who asks you why you believe as you do. Be gentle as you speak and show respect.

1 PETER 3:15

This truth also gives hope of life that lasts forever. God promised this before the world began. He cannot lie.

Titus 1:2

We are waiting for the hope of being made right with God. This will come through the Holy Spirit and by faith.

Galatians 5:5

But Christ was faithful as a Son Who is Head of God's house. We are of God's house if we keep our trust in the Lord until the end. This is our hope.

Hebrews 3:6

God gave these two things that cannot be changed and God cannot lie. We who have turned to Him can have great comfort knowing that He will do what He has promised. This hope is a safe anchor for our souls. It will never move. This hope goes into the Holiest Place of All behind the curtain of heaven.

Hebrews 6:18–19

Our hope comes from God. May He fill you with joy and peace because of your trust in Him. May your hope grow stronger by the power of the Holy Spirit.

Romans 15:13

God wants these great riches of the hidden truth to be made known to the people who are not Jews. The secret is this: Christ in you brings hope of all the great things to come.

Colossians 1:27

Because of Christ, you have put your trust in God. He raised Christ from the dead and gave Him great honor. So now your faith and hope are in God.

1 PETER 1:21

I trust God for the same things they are looking for. I am looking for the dead to rise, both those right with God and the sinful.

ACTS 24:15

We want each one of you to keep on working to the end. Then what you hope for, will happen.

HEBREWS 6:11

But as for me, I will always have hope and I will praise You more and more.

PSALM 71:14

Abraham believed he would be the father of many nations. He had no reason to hope for this, but he had been told, "Your children will become many nations." (Genesis 15:5)

ROMANS 4:18

There is one body and one Spirit. There is one hope in which you were called.

EPHESIANS 4:4

We were saved with this hope ahead of us. Now hope means we are waiting for something we do not have. How can a man hope for something he already has? But if we hope for something we do not yet see, we must learn how to wait for it.

ROMANS 8:24–25

I hope for Your saving power, O Lord, and I follow Your Word.

Psalm 119:166

We speak without fear because our trust is in Christ.

2 Corinthians 3:12

I pray that your hearts will be able to understand. I pray that you will know about the hope given by God's call. I pray that you will see how great the things are that He has promised to those who belong to Him.

Ephesians 1:18

I hope very much that I will have no reason to be ashamed. I hope to honor Christ with my body if it be by my life or by my death. I want to honor Him without fear, now and always.

Philippians 1:20

Remember Your Word to Your servant, for You have given me hope.

Psalm 119:49

Why are you sad, O my soul? Why have you become troubled within me? Hope in God, for I will yet praise Him, my help and my God.

Psalm 42:11

We thank God for the hope that is being kept for you in heaven. You first heard about this hope through the Good News which is the Word of Truth.

Colossians 1:5

We are to be looking for the great hope and the coming of our great God and the One Who saves, Christ Jesus.

TITUS 2:13

Now faith is being sure we will get what we hope for. It is being sure of what we cannot see.

HEBREWS 11:1

But those in need will not always be forgotten. The hope of the poor will not be lost forever.

PSALM 9:18

HOSPITALITY

Just allow your guest to feel at ease because you are, whatever the state of your house. This is an important element to being a gracious host.

LINDA DAVIS ZUMBEHL

Do not forget to be kind to strangers and let them stay in your home. Some people have had angels in their homes without knowing it.

HEBREWS 13:2

" 'If a stranger lives with you in your land, do not do wrong to him. You should act toward the stranger who lives among you as you would toward one born among you. Love him as you love yourself. For you were strangers in the land of Egypt. I am the Lord your God.' "

LEVITICUS 19:33–34

Be happy to have people stay for the night and eat with you.

1 PETER 4:9

A church leader is God's servant. His life must be so that no one can say anything against him. He should not try to please himself and not be quick to get angry over little things. He must not get drunk or want to fight. He must not always want more money for himself. He must like to take people into his home. He must love what is good. He must be able to think well and do all things in the right way. He must live a holy life and be the boss over his own desires.

TITUS 1:7–8

Wisdom has built her house. She has made seven pillars to hold it up. She has cooked her food, and has mixed her wine, and she has set her table. She has sent out the young women who work for her. She calls from the highest places of the city, "Whoever is easy to fool, let him turn in here!" She says to the one without understanding, "Come and eat my food, and drink the wine I have mixed."

PROVERBS 9:1–5

Share what you have with Christian brothers who are in need. Give meals and a place to stay to those who need it.

ROMANS 12:13

"When you have a supper, ask poor people. Ask those who cannot walk and those who are blind. You will be happy if you do this. They cannot pay you back. You will get your pay when the people who are right with God are raised from the dead."

LUKE 14:13–14

She must be known for doing good things for people and for being a good mother. She must be known for taking strangers into her home and for washing the feet of Christians. She must be known for helping those who suffer and for showing kindness.

1 TIMOTHY 5:10

" 'Do not gather what is left among your vines, or gather the grapes that have fallen. Leave them for those in need and for the stranger. I am the Lord your God.' "

LEVITICUS 19:10

What if a Christian does not have clothes or food? And one of you says to him, "Goodbye, keep yourself warm and eat well." But if you do not give him what he needs, how does that help him?

JAMES 2:15–16

"Then the King will say to those on His right side, 'Come, you who have been called by My Father. Come into the holy nation that has been made ready for you before the world was made. For I was hungry and you gave Me food to eat. I was thirsty and you gave Me water to drink. I was a stranger and you gave Me a room. I had no clothes and you gave Me clothes to wear. I was sick and you cared for Me. I was in prison and you came to see Me.' . . .Then the King will say, 'For sure, I tell you, because you did it to one of the least of My brothers, you have done it to Me.' "

MATTHEW 25:34–36, 40

"He does what is right and fair for the child without parents and the woman whose husband has died. He shows His love for the stranger by giving him food and clothing."
DEUTERONOMY 10:18

"For sure, I tell you, whoever gives you a cup of water to drink in My name because you belong to Christ will not lose his reward from God."

MARK 9:41

HUMILITY

All of the charm and beauty a woman may have amounts to nothing if her ambitions are self-centered. But if she reflects her Creator and assumes the posture of a graceful servant, she cannot help but command high respect and love.
JEANNE HENDRICKS

Live in peace with each other. Do not act or think with pride. Be happy to be with poor people. Keep yourself from thinking you are so wise.

ROMANS 12:16

The Lord says, "Let not a wise man speak with pride about his wisdom. Let not the strong man speak with pride about his strength. And let not a rich man speak with pride about his riches."

JEREMIAH 9:23

If I must talk about myself, I will do it about the things that show how weak I am.

2 CORINTHIANS 11:30

"Whoever is without pride as this little child is the greatest in the holy nation of heaven."

MATTHEW 18:4

In the same way, you younger men must obey the church leaders. Be gentle as you care for each other. God works against those who have pride. He gives His loving-favor to those who do not try to honor themselves. So put away all pride from yourselves. You are standing under the powerful hand of God. At the right time He will lift you up.

1 PETER 5:5–6

The fear of the Lord is the teaching for wisdom, and having no pride comes before honor.

PROVERBS 15:33

O Lord, my heart is not proud. My eyes are not filled with pride. And I do not trouble myself with important things or in things too great for me.

PSALM 131:1

The reward for not having pride and having the fear of the Lord is riches, honor and life.

PROVERBS 22:4

"Those who know there is nothing good in themselves are happy, because the holy nation of heaven is theirs."

MATTHEW 5:3

"Listen to me, you who are following what is right and good, and who are looking for the Lord. Look to the rock from which you were cut out, and to the hole from which you were dug."

ISAIAH 51:1

O Lord, You have heard the prayers of those who have no pride. You will give strength to their heart, and You will listen to them.

PSALM 10:17

God makes fun of those who make fun of the truth but gives loving-favor to those who have no pride.

PROVERBS 3:34

"The person who thinks he is important will find out how little he is worth. The person who is not trying to honor himself will be made important."

MATTHEW 23:12

For even if the Lord is honored, He thinks about those who have no pride. But He knows the proud from far away.

PSALM 138:6

For the high and honored One Who lives forever, Whose name is Holy, says, "I live in the high and holy place. And I also live with those who are sorry for their sins and have turned from them and are not proud. I give new strength to the spirit of those without pride, and also to those whose hearts are sorry for their sins.

ISAIAH 57:15

He put aside everything that belonged to Him and made Himself the same as a servant who is owned by someone. He became human by being born as a man. After He became a man, He gave up His important place and obeyed by dying on a cross. Because of this, God lifted Jesus high above everything else. He gave Him a name that is greater than any other name.

PHILIPPIANS 2:7–9

When pride comes, then comes shame, but wisdom is with those who have no pride.

PROVERBS 11:2

For He Who punishes for the blood of another remembers them. He does not forget the cry of those who suffer.

PSALM 9:12

Let yourself be brought low before the Lord. Then He will lift you up and help you.

JAMES 4:10

It is better to be poor in spirit among poor people, than to divide the riches that were taken with the proud.

PROVERBS 16:19

Let another man praise you, and not your own mouth. Let a stranger, and not your own lips.

PROVERBS 27:2

Do not hurry to speak or be in a hurry as you think what to tell God. For God is in heaven and you are on the earth. So let your words be few.

ECCLESIASTES 5:2

Joy

Laughter lightens the load.
Patsy Clairmont

The angel said to them, "Do not be afraid. See! I bring you good news of great joy which is for all people."
Luke 2:10

The Lord is my strength and my safe cover. My heart trusts in Him, and I am helped. So my heart is full of joy. I will thank Him with my song.
Psalm 28:7

Be full of joy always because you belong to the Lord. Again I say, be full of joy!
Philippians 4:4

"Until now you have not asked for anything in My name. Ask and you will receive. Then your joy will be full."
John 16:24

Be glad in the Lord and be full of joy, you who are right with God! Sing for joy all you who are pure in heart!
Psalm 32:11

A sinful man is trapped by his sins, but a man who is right with God sings for joy.
Proverbs 29:6

We are full of sorrow and yet we are always happy. We are poor and yet we make many people rich. We have nothing and yet we have everything.

2 CORINTHIANS 6:10

My lips will call out for joy when I sing praises to You. You have set my soul free.

PSALM 71:23

A glad heart is good medicine, but a broken spirit dries up the bones.

PROVERBS 17:22

So the people, for whom the Lord paid the price to be saved, will return. They will come with songs of joy to Zion. Joy that lasts forever will be on their heads. They will receive joy and happiness, and sorrow and sad voices will hurry away.

ISAIAH 51:11

"His owner said to him, 'You have done well. You are a good and faithful servant. You have been faithful over a few things. I will put many things in your care. Come and share my joy.' "

MATTHEW 25:21

"Be glad in that day. Be full of joy for your reward is much in heaven. Their fathers did these things to the early preachers."

LUKE 6:23

Call out with joy to the Lord, all the earth. Be glad as you serve the Lord. Come before Him with songs of joy.

PSALM 100:1–2

"But now I come to You, Father. I say these things while I am in the world. In this way, My followers may have My joy in their hearts."

JOHN 17:13

All the days of the suffering are hard, but a glad heart has a special supper all the time.

PROVERBS 15:15

But let all who look for You have joy and be glad in You. Let those who love Your saving power always say, "The Lord be honored!"

PSALM 40:16

Not only that, we give thanks to God through our Lord Jesus Christ. Through Him we have been brought back to God.

ROMANS 5:11

We are not the boss of your faith but we are working with you to make you happy. Your faith is strong.

2 CORINTHIANS 1:24

Is anyone among you suffering? He should pray. Is anyone happy? He should sing songs of thanks to God.

JAMES 5:13

For our heart is full of joy in Him, because we trust in His holy name.

PSALM 33:21

Tell of your joy to each other by singing the Songs of David and church songs. Sing in your heart to the Lord.

EPHESIANS 5:19

I will have much joy in the Lord. My soul will have joy in my God, for He has clothed me with the clothes of His saving power. He has put around me a coat of what is right and good, as a man at his own wedding wears something special on his head, and as a bride makes herself beautiful with stones of great worth.

ISAIAH 61:10

KINDNESS

Let no one ever come to you without leaving better and happier. Be the living expression of God's kindness: kindness in your face, kindness in your eyes, kindness in your smile.

MOTHER TERESA

"Give to any person who asks you for something. If a person takes something from you, do not ask for it back."

LUKE 6:30

When someone does something bad to you, do not do the same thing to him. When someone talks about you, do not talk about him. Instead, pray that good will come to him. You were called to do this so you might receive good things from God.

1 PETER 3:9

She opens her mouth with wisdom. The teaching of kindness is on her tongue.

PROVERBS 31:26

God has chosen you. You are holy and loved by Him. Because of this, your new life should be full of loving-pity. You should be kind to others and have no pride. Be gentle and be willing to wait for others.

COLOSSIANS 3:12

As you live God-like, be kind to Christian brothers and love them. If you have all these things and keep growing in them, they will keep you from being of no use and from having no fruit when it comes to knowing our Lord Jesus Christ.

2 PETER 1:7–8

Each of us should live to please his neighbor. This will help him grow in faith.

ROMANS 15:2

"The Lord of All said, 'Do what is right and be kind and show loving-pity to one another. Do not make it hard for the woman whose husband has died, or the child who has no parents, or the stranger, or the poor. Do not make sinful plans in your hearts against one another.' "

ZECHARIAH 7:9–10

"If you let people use your things and expect to get something back, what pay can you expect from that? Even sinners let sinners use things and they expect to get something back. But love those who hate you. Do good to them. Let them use your things and do not expect something back. Your reward will be much. You will be the children of the Most High. He is kind to those who are not thankful and to those who are full of sin."

LUKE 6:34–35

Be happy with those who are happy. Be sad with those who are sad.

ROMANS 12:15

Do not let yourselves get tired of doing good. If we do not give up, we will get what is coming to us at the right time. Because of this, we should do good to everyone. For sure, we should do good to those who belong to Christ.

GALATIANS 6:9–10

He who hates his neighbor sins, but happy is he who shows loving-favor to the poor.

PROVERBS 14:21

"Give to any person who asks you for something. Do not say no to the man who wants to use something of yours."

MATTHEW 5:42

And Boaz said, "May the Lord bring good to you, my daughter. You have shown your last kindness to be better than your first by not going after young men, with or without riches. Now my daughter, do not be afraid. I will do for you whatever you ask. For all my people in the city know that you are a good woman."

RUTH 3:10–11

What is desired in a man is his kindness, and it is better to be a poor man than a liar.

PROVERBS 19:22

Everything we do shows we are God's servants. We have had to wait and suffer. We have needed things. We have been in many hard places and have had many troubles. . . . We have been pure. We have known what to do. We have suffered long. We have been kind. The Holy Spirit has worked in us. We have had true love. . . . We are full of sorrow and yet we are always happy. We are poor and yet we make many people rich. We have nothing and yet we have everything.

2 CORINTHIANS 6:4, 6, 10

LOVE FOR OTHERS

If I put my own good name before the other's highest good, then I know nothing of Calvary love.

AMY CARMICHAEL

Love each other as Christian brothers. Show respect for each other.

ROMANS 12:10

You do not need anyone to write to you about loving your Christian brothers. God has taught you to love each other.

1 THESSALONIANS 4:9

Christian brother, you were chosen to be free. Be careful that you do not please your old selves by sinning because you are free. Live this free life by loving and helping others. You obey the whole Law when you do this one thing, "Love your neighbor as you love yourself." (Leviticus 19:18)

GALATIANS 5:13–14

As you live God-like, be kind to Christian brothers and love them.

2 PETER 1:7

Dear friends, if God loved us that much, then we should love each other. No person has ever seen God at any time. If we love each other, God lives in us. His love is made perfect in us.

1 JOHN 4:11–12

And now we have these three: faith and hope and love, but the greatest of these is love.

1 CORINTHIANS 13:13

"You have heard that it has been said, 'You must love your neighbor and hate those who hate you.' But I tell you, love those who hate you. (*Respect and give thanks for those who say bad things to you. Do good to those who hate you.) Pray for those who do bad things to you and who make it hard for you. Then you may be the sons of your Father Who is in heaven. His sun shines on bad people and on good people. He sends rain on those who are right with God and on those who are not right with God."

MATTHEW 5:43–45

This is what you have heard from the beginning, that we should love each other.

1 John 3:11

Do not hurt someone who has hurt you. Do not keep on hating the sons of your people, but love your neighbor as yourself. I am the Lord.

Leviticus 19:18

I may be able to speak the languages of men and even of angels, but if I do not have love, it will sound like noisy brass. If I have the gift of speaking God's Word and if I understand all secrets, but do not have love, I am nothing. If I know all things and if I have the gift of faith so I can move mountains, but do not have love, I am nothing. If I give everything I have to feed poor people and if I give my body to be burned, but do not have love, it will not help me.

1 Corinthians 13:1–3

Do not owe anyone anything, but love each other. Whoever loves his neighbor has done what the Law says to do.

Romans 13:8

Let us help each other to love others and to do good.

Hebrews 10:24

This is the way you can know who are the children of God and who are the children of the devil. The person who does not keep on doing what is right and does not love his brother does not belong to God.

1 John 3:10

You may make the weak Christian fall into sin by what you have done. Remember, he is a Christian brother for whom Christ died. When you sin against a weak Christian by making him do what is wrong, you sin against Christ.

1 Corinthians 8:11–12

Those who do not love do not know God because God is love.

1 John 4:8

"This is what I tell you to do: Love each other just as I have loved you. No one can have greater love than to give his life for his friends."

John 15:12–13

You should be ashamed! Is it true that there is not one person wise enough in your church to decide who is right when people argue? Instead, one Christian takes another Christian to court. And that court is made up of people who are not Christians! This shows you are wrong when you have to go to court against each other. Would it not be better to let someone do something against you that is wrong? Would it not be better to let them rob you? Instead, you rob and do wrong to other Christians.

1 Corinthians 6:5–8

If a person says, "I love God," but hates his brother, he is a liar. If a person does not love his brother whom he has seen, how can he love God Whom he has not seen? We have these words from Him. If you love God, love your brother also.

1 John 4:20–21

Leave your gift on the altar. Go and make right what is wrong between you and him. Then come back and give your gift.

MATTHEW 5:24

You have made your souls pure by obeying the truth through the Holy Spirit. This has given you a true love for the Christians. Let it be a true love from the heart.

1 PETER 1:22

Show respect to all men. Love the Christians. Honor God with love and fear. Respect the head leader of the country.

1 PETER 2:17

And this is my prayer: I pray that your love will grow more and more. I pray that you will have better understanding and be wise in all things.

PHILIPPIANS 1:9

We know what love is because Christ gave His life for us. We should give our lives for our brothers. What if a person has enough money to live on and sees his brother in need of food and clothing? If he does not help him, how can the love of God be in him? My children, let us not love with words or in talk only. Let us love by what we do and in truth. This is how we know we are Christians. It will give our heart comfort for sure when we stand before Him.

1 JOHN 3:16–19

"I give you a new Law. You are to love each other. You must love each other as I have loved you. If you love each other, all men will know you are My followers."

JOHN 13:34–35

Dear friends, let us love each other, because love comes from God. Those who love are God's children and they know God. Those who do not love do not know God because God is love. God has shown His love to us by sending His only Son into the world. God did this so we might have life through Christ. This is love! It is not that we loved God but that He loved us. For God sent His Son to pay for our sins with His own blood. Dear friends, if God loved us that much, then we should love each other.

1 JOHN 4:7–11

Last of all, you must share the same thoughts and the same feelings. Love each other with a kind heart and with a mind that has no pride.

1 PETER 3:8

LOVE OF GOD

The greatest need in the world today
is love. . . . More love for each other
and more love for God above!
HELEN STEINER RICE

The Lord takes care of all who love Him.

PSALM 145:20

Be very careful to love the Lord your God.

JOSHUA 23:11

Know then that the Lord your God is God, the faithful God. He keeps His promise and shows His loving-kindness to those who love Him and keep His Laws, even to a thousand family groups in the future.

DEUTERONOMY 7:9

Jesus said to him, "The greatest Law is this, 'Listen, Jewish people, The Lord our God is one Lord! You must love the Lord your God with all your heart and with all your soul and with all your mind and with all your strength.' (Deuteronomy 6:4–5) This is the first Law. The second Law is this: 'You must love your neighbor as yourself.' (Leviticus 19:18) No other Law is greater than these."

MARK 12:29–31

The Lord came to us from far away, saying, "I have loved you with a love that lasts forever. So I have helped you come to Me with loving-kindness."

JEREMIAH 31:3

But if he loves God, he is known by God also.

1 CORINTHIANS 8:3

I pray that Christ may live in your hearts by faith. I pray that you will be filled with love. I pray that you will be able to understand how wide and how long and how high and how deep His love is. I pray that you will know the love of Christ. His love goes beyond anything we can understand. I pray that you will be filled with God Himself.

EPHESIANS 3:17–19

"I have loved you just as My Father has loved Me. Stay in My love."

JOHN 15:9

Jesus said to them, "If God were your father, you would love Me. I came from God. I did not come on My own, but God sent Me."

JOHN 8:42

God always does what is right. He will not forget the work you did to help the Christians and the work you are still doing to help them. This shows your love for Christ.

HEBREWS 6:10

And you must love the Lord your God with all your heart and with all your soul and with all your strength.

DEUTERONOMY 6:5

Do not love the world or anything in the world. If anyone loves the world, the Father's love is not in him.

1 JOHN 2:15

"I love those who love me, and those who look for me with much desire will find me."

PROVERBS 8:17

Be happy in the Lord. And He will give you the desires of your heart.

PSALM 37:4

We know that God makes all things work together for the good of those who love Him and are chosen to be a part of His plan.

ROMANS 8:28

I will make Your name known to my brothers. In the center of the meeting of worship I will praise You.

PSALM 22:22

"I have made Your name known to them and will make it known. So then the love You have for Me may be in them and I may be in them."

JOHN 17:26

Keep yourselves in the love of God. Wait for life that lasts forever through the loving-kindness of our Lord Jesus Christ.

JUDE 21

We have come to know and believe the love God has for us. God is love. If you live in love, you live by the help of God and God lives in you. Love is made perfect in us when we are not ashamed as we stand before Him on the day He judges. For we know that our life in this world is His life lived in us. There is no fear in love. Perfect love puts fear out of our hearts. People have fear when they are afraid of being punished. The man who is afraid does not have perfect love. We love Him because He loved us first.

1 JOHN 4:16–19

"The one who loves Me is the one who has My teaching and obeys it. My Father will love whoever loves Me. I will love him and will show Myself to him."

JOHN 14:21

Mercy

God deals with us from a merciful posture;
His arms are open, His words are healing,
He wants sinners to return to Him.
Martie Stowell

"You must have loving-kindness just as your Father has loving-kindness."

Luke 6:36

But You, O Lord, are a God full of love and pity. You are slow to anger and rich in loving-kindness and truth.

Psalm 86:15

So return to your God. Show kindness and do what is fair, and wait for your God all the time.

Hosea 12:6

"Those who show loving-kindness are happy, because they will have loving-kindness shown to them."

Matthew 5:7

We think of those who stayed true to Him as happy even though they suffered. You have heard how long Job waited. You have seen what the Lord did for him in the end. The Lord is full of loving-kindness and pity.

James 5:11

For You are good and ready to forgive, O Lord. You are rich in loving-kindness to all who call to You.

PSALM 86:5

O man, He has told you what is good. What does the Lord ask of you but to do what is fair and to love kindness, and to walk without pride with your God?

MICAH 6:8

Let us thank the God and Father of our Lord Jesus Christ. It was through His loving-kindness that we were born again to a new life and have a hope that never dies. This hope is ours because Jesus was raised from the dead.

1 PETER 1:3

They would not listen, and did not remember Your powerful works which You had done among them. So they became strong-willed and chose a leader to return to their hard work in Egypt. But You are a forgiving God. You are kind and loving, slow to anger, and full of loving-kindness. You did not leave them.

NEHEMIAH 9:17

God has said that all men have broken His Law. But He will show loving-kindness on all of them.

ROMANS 11:32

The Lord is good to all. And His loving-kindness is over all His works.

PSALM 145:9

Do not let kindness and truth leave you. Tie them around your neck. Write them upon your heart. So you will find favor and good understanding in the eyes of God and man.

PROVERBS 3:3–4

It will not go well for the man who hides his sins, but he who tells his sins and turns from them will be given loving-pity.

PROVERBS 28:13

But God had so much loving-kindness. He loved us with such a great love. Even when we were dead because of our sins, He made us alive by what Christ did for us. You have been saved from the punishment of sin by His loving-favor.

EPHESIANS 2:4–5

But God, the One Who saves, showed how kind He was and how He loved us by saving us from the punishment of sin. It was not because we worked to be right with God. It was because of His loving-kindness that He washed our sins away. At the same time He gave us new life when the Holy Spirit came into our lives. God gave the Holy Spirit to fill our lives through Jesus Christ, the One Who saves. Because of this, we are made right with God by His loving-favor. Now we can have life that lasts forever as He has promised.

TITUS 3:4–7

Let the sinful turn from his way, and the one who does not know God turn from his thoughts. Let him turn to the Lord, and He will have loving-pity on him. Let him turn to our God, for He will for sure forgive all his sins.

ISAIAH 55:7

Loving-kindness and truth have met together. Peace and what is right and good have kissed each other.

PSALM 85:10

"I will show loving-kindness to them and forgive their sins. I will remember their sins no more." (Jeremiah 31:31–34) When God spoke about a New Way of Worship, He showed that the Old Way of Worship was finished and of no use now. It will never be used again.

HEBREWS 8:12–13

The loving-kindness of the Lord is given to the people of all times who honor Him.

LUKE 1:50

MODESTY

A woman with a gentle and quiet spirit is not only precious to God, but she is attractive to others also. She dresses appropriately, but it is her inner adornment that is noted because she is secure and at rest within her spirit.

CYNTHIA HEALD

God has chosen what is weak and foolish of the world, what is hated and not known, to destroy the things the world trusts in. In that way, no man can be proud as he stands before God.

1 CORINTHIANS 1:28–29

Christian women should not be dressed in the kind of clothes and their hair should not be combed in a way that will make people look at them. They should not wear much gold or pearls or clothes that cost much money. Instead of these things, Christian women should be known for doing good things and living good lives.

1 TIMOTHY 2:9–10

Do not fool yourself. If anyone thinks he knows a lot about the things of this world, he had better become a fool. Then he may become wise.

1 CORINTHIANS 3:18

Do not let your beauty come from the outside. It should not be the way you comb your hair or the wearing of gold or the wearing of fine clothes. Your beauty should come from the inside. It should come from the heart. This is the kind that lasts. Your beauty should be a gentle and quiet spirit. In God's sight this is of great worth and no amount of money can buy it.

1 PETER 3:3–4

But instead you are proud. You talk loud and big about yourselves. All such pride is sin.

JAMES 4:16

A man's pride will bring him down, but he whose spirit is without pride will receive honor.

PROVERBS 29:23

Let another man praise you, and not your own mouth. Let a stranger, and not your own lips.

PROVERBS 27:2

Teach older women to be quiet and to be careful how they act also. They are not to go around speaking bad things about others or things that are not true. They are not to be chained by strong drink. They should teach what is good. Older women are to teach the young women to love their husbands and children. They are to teach them to think before they act, to be pure, to be workers at home, to be kind, and to obey their own husbands. In this way, the Word of God is honored.

TITUS 2:3–5

OBEDIENCE

The only way I will keep a pliable, obedient spirit in the larger decisions is to look to Him and to obey in the smaller ones.
CATHERINE MARSHALL

Now then, if you will obey My voice and keep My agreement, you will belong to Me from among all nations. For all the earth is Mine.

EXODUS 19:5

Keep His Laws which I am giving you today. Then it may go well with you and your children after you. And you may live long in the land the Lord your God is giving you for all time.

DEUTERONOMY 4:40

Be careful to listen to all these words I am telling you. Then it will go well with you and your children after you forever. For you will be doing what is good and right in the eyes of the Lord your God.

DEUTERONOMY 12:28

My son, do not forget my teaching. Let your heart keep my words. For they will add to you many days and years of life and peace.

PROVERBS 3:1–2

But the one who keeps looking into God's perfect Law and does not forget it will do what it says and be happy as he does it. God's Word makes men free.

JAMES 1:25

Keep on doing all the things you learned and received and heard from me. Do the things you saw me do. Then the God Who gives peace will be with you.

PHILIPPIANS 4:9

"Not everyone who says to me, 'Lord, Lord,' will go into the holy nation of heaven. The one who does the things My Father in heaven wants him to do will go into the holy nation of heaven."

MATTHEW 7:21

I tell you today to love the Lord your God. Walk in His ways. Keep all His Laws and all that He has decided. Then you will live and become many. And the Lord your God will bring good to you in the land you are going in to take.

DEUTERONOMY 30:16

The last word, after all has been heard, is: Honor God and obey His Laws. This is all that every person must do.

ECCLESIASTES 12:13

"If you obey My teaching, you will live in My love. In this way, I have obeyed My Father's teaching and live in His love."

JOHN 15:10

All the paths of the Lord are loving and true for those who keep His agreement and keep His Laws.

PSALM 25:10

Samuel said, "Is the Lord pleased as much with burnt gifts as He is when He is obeyed? See, it is better to obey than to give gifts. It is better to listen than to give the fat of rams.

1 SAMUEL 15:22

"Anyone who breaks even the least of the Law of Moses and teaches people not to do what it says, will be called the least in the holy nation of heaven. He who obeys and teaches others to obey what the Law of Moses says, will be called great in the holy nation of heaven."

MATTHEW 5:19

Just to hear the Law does not make a man right with God. The man right with God is the one who obeys the Law.

ROMANS 2:13

The world and all its desires will pass away. But the man who obeys God and does what He wants done will live forever.

1 JOHN 2:17

But He said, "Yes, but those who hear the Word of God and obey it are happy."

LUKE 11:28

So be careful to keep the words of this agreement and obey them so all that you do will go well.

DEUTERONOMY 29:9

Remember that our fathers on earth punished us. We had respect for them. How much more should we obey our Father in heaven and live?

HEBREWS 12:9

Happy are those who keep His Law and look for Him with all their heart.

PSALM 119:2

My Christian friends, you have obeyed me when I was with you. You have obeyed even more when I have been away. You must keep on working to show you have been saved from the punishment of sin. Be afraid that you may not please God.

PHILIPPIANS 2:12

If you are willing and obey, you will eat the best of the land.

ISAIAH 1:19

Patience

Obedience is the fruit of faith;
patience, the bloom on the fruit.
Christina Rossetti

A servant owned by God must not make trouble. He must be kind to everyone. He must be able to teach. He must be willing to suffer when hurt for doing good.
2 Timothy 2:24

Rest in the Lord and be willing to wait for Him. Do not trouble yourself when all goes well with the one who carries out his sinful plans. Stop being angry. Turn away from fighting. Do not trouble yourself. It leads only to wrong-doing. For those who do wrong will be cut off. But those who wait for the Lord will be given the earth.
Psalm 37:7–9

You must be willing to wait without giving up. After you have done what God wants you to do, God will give you what He promised you.
Hebrews 10:36

You know these prove your faith. It helps you not to give up. Learn well how to wait so you will be strong and complete and in need of nothing.

JAMES 1:3–4

"But those which fell on good ground have heard the Word. They keep it in a good and true heart and they keep on giving good grain."

LUKE 8:15

Do not let yourselves get tired of doing good. If we do not give up, we will get what is coming to us at the right time.

GALATIANS 6:9

We are glad for our troubles also. We know that troubles help us learn not to give up. When we have learned not to give up, it shows we have stood the test. When we have stood the test, it gives us hope.

ROMANS 5:3–4

Everything we do shows we are God's servants. We have had to wait and suffer. We have needed things. We have been in many hard places and have had many troubles.

2 CORINTHIANS 6:4

We ask you, Christian brothers, speak to those who do not want to work. Comfort those who feel they cannot keep going on. Help the weak. Understand and be willing to wait for all men.

1 THESSALONIANS 5:14

Everything that was written in the Holy Writings long ago was written to teach us. By not giving up, God's Word gives us strength and hope. Now the God Who helps you not to give up and gives you strength will help you think so you can please each other as Christ Jesus did.

ROMANS 15:4–5

May the Lord lead your hearts into the love of God. May He help you as you wait for Christ.

2 THESSALONIANS 3:5

Christian brothers, be willing to wait for the Lord to come again. Learn from the farmer. He waits for the good fruit from the earth until the early and late rains come. You must be willing to wait also. Be strong in your hearts because the Lord is coming again soon.

JAMES 5:7–8

All these many people who have had faith in God are around us like a cloud. Let us put every thing out of our lives that keeps us from doing what we should. Let us keep running in the race that God has planned for us.

HEBREWS 12:1

Do not be lazy. Be like those who have faith and have not given up. They will receive what God has promised them.

HEBREWS 6:12

What good is it if, when you are beaten for doing something wrong, you do not try to get out of it? But if you are beaten when you have done what is right, and do not try to get out of it, God is pleased.

1 PETER 2:20

The end of something is better than its beginning. Not giving up in spirit is better than being proud in spirit. Do not be quick in spirit to be angry. For anger is in the heart of fools.

ECCLESIASTES 7:8–9

Abraham was willing to wait and God gave to him what He had promised.

HEBREWS 6:15

Those who keep on doing good and are looking for His greatness and honor will receive life that lasts forever.

ROMANS 2:7

"But stay true and your souls will have life."

LUKE 21:19

PEACE

Like a river glorious is God's perfect peace.
Over all victorious in its bright increase;
Perfect, yet it floweth fuller every day,
Perfect, yet it groweth deeper all the way.
Stayed upon Jehovah, hearts are fully blest;
Finding, as He promised, perfect peace and rest.
FRANCES RIDLEY HAVERGAL

"The mountains may be taken away and the hills may shake, but My loving-kindness will not be taken from you. And My agreement of peace will not be shaken," says the Lord who has loving-pity on you. . . . All your sons will be taught by the Lord, and the well-being of your children will be great.

Isaiah 54:10, 13

Our hope comes from God. May He fill you with joy and peace because of your trust in Him. May your hope grow stronger by the power of the Holy Spirit.

Romans 15:13

The Lord will give strength to His people. The Lord will give His people peace.

Psalm 29:11

When the ways of a man are pleasing to the Lord, He makes even those who hate him to be at peace with him.

Proverbs 16:7

Those who make peace are happy, because they will be called the sons of God.

Matthew 5:9

Lying is in the heart of those who plan what is bad, but those who plan peace have joy.

Proverbs 12:20

Those who plant seeds of peace will gather what is right and good.

James 3:18

Work hard to live together as one by the help of the Holy Spirit. Then there will be peace.

EPHESIANS 4:3

"Greatness and honor to our God in the highest heaven and peace on earth among men who please Him."

LUKE 2:14

Turn away from the sinful things young people want to do. Go after what is right. Have a desire for faith and love and peace. Do this with those who pray to God from a clean heart.

2 TIMOTHY 2:22

Look at the man without blame. And watch the man who is right and good. For the man of peace will have much family to follow him.

PSALM 37:37

As much as you can, live in peace with all men.

ROMANS 12:18

He will judge between the nations, and will decide for many people. And they will beat their swords into plows, and their spears into knives for cutting vines. Nation will not lift up sword against nation, and they will not learn about war anymore.

ISAIAH 2:4

The peace of God is much greater than the human mind can understand. This peace will keep your hearts and minds through Christ Jesus.

PHILIPPIANS 4:7

First of all, I ask you to pray much for all men and to give thanks for them. Pray for kings and all others who are in power over us so we might live quiet God-like lives in peace.

1 TIMOTHY 2:1–2

Be at peace with all men. Live a holy life. No one will see the Lord without having that kind of life.

HEBREWS 12:14

See, how good and how pleasing it is for brothers to live together as one!

PSALM 133:1

For "If you want joy in your life and have happy days, keep your tongue from saying bad things and your lips from talking bad about others. Turn away from what is sinful. Do what is good. Look for peace and go after it."

1 PETER 3:10–11

You will keep the man in perfect peace whose mind is kept on You, because he trusts in You.

ISAIAH 26:3

For God did not give us a spirit of fear. He gave us a spirit of power and of love and of a good mind.

2 TIMOTHY 1:7

"Peace I leave with you. My peace I give to you. I do not give peace to you as the world gives. Do not let your hearts be troubled or afraid."

JOHN 14:27

Perseverance

You may have to fight a battle more than once to win it.
Margaret Thatcher

For this reason, I am suffering. But I am not ashamed. I know the One in Whom I have put my trust. I am sure He is able to keep safe that which I have trusted to Him until the day He comes again. Keep all the things I taught you. They were given to you in the faith and love of Jesus Christ.

2 Timothy 1:12–13

For we belong to Christ if we keep on trusting Him to the end just as we trusted Him at first.

Hebrews 3:14

These tests have come to prove your faith and to show that it is good. Gold, which can be destroyed, is tested by fire. Your faith is worth much more than gold and it must be tested also. Then your faith will bring thanks and shining-greatness and honor to Jesus Christ when He comes again.

1 Peter 1:7

Take your share of suffering as a good soldier of Jesus Christ.

2 Timothy 2:3

You must pray at all times as the Holy Spirit leads you to pray. Pray for the things that are needed. You must watch and keep on praying. Remember to pray for all Christians.

EPHESIANS 6:18

We are taught to have nothing to do with that which is against God. We are to have nothing to do with the desires of this world. We are to be wise and to be right with God. We are to live God-like lives in this world. We are to be looking for the great hope and the coming of our great God and the One Who saves, Christ Jesus.

TITUS 2:12–13

When he falls, he will not be thrown down, because the Lord holds his hand.

PSALM 37:24

Let us hold on to the hope we say we have and not be changed. We can trust God that He will do what He promised.

HEBREWS 10:23

For I know that nothing can keep us from the love of God. Death cannot! Life cannot! Angels cannot! Leaders cannot! Any other power cannot! Hard things now or in the future cannot! The world above or the world below cannot! Any other living thing cannot keep us away from the love of God which is ours through Christ Jesus our Lord.

ROMANS 8:38–39

Christ made us free. Stay that way. Do not get chained all over again in the Law and its kind of religious worship.

GALATIANS 5:1

But the way of those who are right is like the early morning light. It shines brighter and brighter until the perfect day.

PROVERBS 4:18

He said to the Jews who believed, "If you keep and obey My Word, then you are My followers for sure."

JOHN 8:31

And so, dear friends, now that you know this, watch so you will not be led away by the mistakes of these sinful people. Do not be moved by them.

2 PETER 3:17

It is life to us to know that your faith in the Lord is strong.

1 THESSALONIANS 3:8

In each city they helped the Christians to be strong and true to the faith. They told them, "We must suffer many hard things to get into the holy nation of God."

ACTS 14:22

Who can keep us away from the love of Christ? Can trouble or problems? Can suffering wrong from others or having no food? Can it be because of no clothes or because of danger or war?

ROMANS 8:35

Because of this, put on all the things God gives you to fight with. Then you will be able to stand in that sinful day. When it is all over, you will still be standing.

EPHESIANS 6:13

All these many people who have had faith in God are around us like a cloud. Let us put every thing out of our lives that keeps us from doing what we should. Let us keep running in the race that God has planned for us. Let us keep looking to Jesus. Our faith comes from Him and He is the One Who makes it perfect. He did not give up when He had to suffer shame and die on a cross. He knew of the joy that would be His later. Now He is sitting at the right side of God.

HEBREWS 12:1–2

So, my dear Christian brothers, you are my joy and crown. I want to see you. Keep on staying true to the Lord, my dear friends.

PHILIPPIANS 4:1

POWER

The stone still stood there in that quiet garden, a reminder of the reality of the problem we all must live with; but Christ had moved it to one side so very easily, demonstrating His resurrection power on our behalf.

JILL BRISCOE

Look to the Lord and ask for His strength. Look to Him all the time.

1 CHRONICLES 16:11

The Lord your God is with you, a Powerful One Who wins the battle. He will have much joy over you. With His love He will give you new life. He will have joy over you with loud singing.

ZEPHANIAH 3:17

God is able to do much more than we ask or think through His power working in us.

EPHESIANS 3:20

The holy nation of God is not made up of words. It is made up of power.

1 CORINTHIANS 4:20

"But you will receive power when the Holy Spirit comes into your life. You will tell about Me in the city of Jerusalem and over all the countries of Judea and Samaria and to the ends of the earth."

ACTS 1:8

I pray that you will know how great His power is for those who have put their trust in Him. It is the same power that raised Christ from the dead. This same power put Christ at God's right side in heaven.

EPHESIANS 1:19–20

The Good News did not come to you by word only, but with power and through the Holy Spirit. You knew it was true. You also knew how we lived among you. It was for your good.

1 THESSALONIANS 1:5

Christ's weak human body died on a cross. It is by God's power that Christ lives today. We are weak. We are as He was. But we will be alive with Christ through the power God has for us.

2 CORINTHIANS 13:4

PRAYER

Prayer is an indispensable part
of our relationship
with Jesus Christ.
LAUREL OKE LOGAN

"When the time comes that you see Me again, you will ask Me no question. For sure, I tell you, My Father will give you whatever you ask in My name. Until now you have not asked for anything in My name. Ask and you will receive. Then your joy will be full."

JOHN 16:23–24

"When you pray, go into a room by yourself. After you have shut the door, pray to your Father Who is in secret. Then your Father Who sees in secret will reward you. When you pray, do not say the same thing over and over again making long prayers like the people who do not know God. They think they are heard because their prayers are long."

MATTHEW 6:6–7

Hear my words, O Lord. Think about my crying. Listen to my cry for help, my King and my God. For I pray to you. In the morning, O Lord, You will hear my voice. In the morning I will lay my prayers before You and will look up.

PSALM 5:1–3

"Then we will use all of our time to pray and to teach the Word of God."

ACTS 6:4

"You are bad and you know how to give good things to your children. How much more will your Father in heaven give good things to those who ask Him?"

MATTHEW 7:11

Be happy in your hope. Do not give up when trouble comes. Do not let anything stop you from praying.

ROMANS 12:12

I will cry out and complain in the evening and morning and noon, and He will hear my voice.

PSALM 55:17

O people in Zion who live in Jerusalem, you will cry no more. For sure He will show loving-kindness to you at the sound of your cry. When He hears it, He will answer you.

ISAIAH 30:19

In the same way, the Holy Spirit helps us where we are weak. We do not know how to pray or what we should pray for, but the Holy Spirit prays to God for us with sounds that cannot be put into words.

ROMANS 8:26

You must pray at all times as the Holy Spirit leads you to pray. Pray for the things that are needed. You must watch and keep on praying. Remember to pray for all Christians.

EPHESIANS 6:18

I did not give up waiting for the Lord. And He turned to me and heard my cry.

PSALM 40:1

"Will not God make the things that are right come to His chosen people who cry day and night to Him? Will He wait a long time to help them?"

LUKE 18:7

If My people who are called by My name put away their pride and pray, and look for My face, and turn from their sinful ways, then I will hear from heaven. I will forgive their sin, and will heal their land.

2 CHRONICLES 7:14

Then you will call upon Me and come and pray to Me, and I will listen to you.

JEREMIAH 29:12

"All things you ask for in prayer, you will receive if you have faith."

MATTHEW 21:22

The Lord is near to all who call on Him, to all who call on Him in truth.

PSALM 145:18

Let us go with complete trust to the throne of God. We will receive His loving-kindness and have His loving-favor to help us whenever we need it.

HEBREWS 4:16

The Lord hates the gifts of the sinful, but the prayer of the faithful is His joy.

PROVERBS 15:8

"Ask, and what you are asking for will be given to you. Look, and what you are looking for you will find. Knock, and the door you are knocking on will be opened to you. Everyone who asks receives what he asks for. Everyone who looks finds what he is looking for. Everyone who knocks has the door opened to him."

MATTHEW 7:7–8

And it will be before they call, I will answer. While they are still speaking, I will hear.

ISAIAH 65:24

Tell your sins to each other. And pray for each other so you may be healed. The prayer from the heart of a man right with God has much power.

JAMES 5:16

We are sure that if we ask anything that He wants us to have, He will hear us. If we are sure He hears us when we ask, we can be sure He will give us what we ask for.

1 JOHN 5:14–15

Never stop praying.

1 THESSALONIANS 5:17

I want men everywhere to pray. They should lift up holy hands as they pray. They should not be angry or argue.

1 TIMOTHY 2:8

Let them give thanks to the Lord for His loving-kindness and His great works to the children of men!

PSALM 107:15

What should I do? I will pray with my spirit and I will pray with my mind also. I will sing with my spirit and I will sing with my mind also.

1 CORINTHIANS 14:15

The Lord will send His loving-kindness in the day. And His song will be with me in the night, a prayer to the God of my life.

PSALM 42:8

"Again I tell you this: If two of you agree on earth about anything you pray for, it will be done for you by My Father in heaven. For where two or three are gathered together in My name, there I am with them."

MATTHEW 18:19–20

He will call upon Me, and I will answer him. I will be with him in trouble. I will take him out of trouble and honor him.

PSALM 91:15

I will call on Him as long as I live, because He has turned His ear to me.

PSALM 116:2

Is anyone among you suffering? He should pray. Is anyone happy? He should sing songs of thanks to God. Is anyone among you sick? He should send for the church leaders and they should pray for him. They should pour oil on him in the name of the Lord. The prayer given in faith will heal the sick man, and the Lord will raise him up. If he has sinned, he will be forgiven.

JAMES 5:13–15

Do not worry. Learn to pray about everything. Give thanks to God as you ask Him for what you need. The peace of God is much greater than the human mind can understand. This peace will keep your hearts and minds through Christ Jesus.

PHILIPPIANS 4:6–7

PRIDE

Why are we not far more frightened of what pride can do?
Pride can cost us—and probably those after us.
BETH MOORE

Do not be wise in your own eyes. Fear the Lord and turn away from what is sinful.

PROVERBS 3:7

Jesus sat down and called the followers to Him. He said, "If anyone wants to be first, he must be last of all. He will be the one to care for all."

MARK 9:35

Eyes lifted high and a proud heart is sin and is the lamp of the sinful.

PROVERBS 21:4

But instead you are proud. You talk loud and big about yourselves. All such pride is sin.

JAMES 4:16

Live in peace with each other. Do not act or think with pride. Be happy to be with poor people. Keep yourself from thinking you are so wise.

ROMANS 12:16

Speak no more in your pride. Do not let proud talk come out of your mouth. For the Lord is a God Who knows. Actions are weighed by Him.

1 SAMUEL 2:3

The fear of the Lord is to hate what is sinful. I hate pride, self-love, the way of sin, and lies.

PROVERBS 8:13

Jesus said to them, "You are the kind of people who make yourselves look good before other people. God knows your hearts. What men think is good is hated in the eyes of God."

LUKE 16:15

Do not let the foot of pride come near me. Do not let the hand of the sinful push me away.

PSALM 36:11

A proud man starts fights, but all will go well for the man who trusts in the Lord. He who trusts in his own heart is a fool, but he who walks in wisdom will be kept safe.

PROVERBS 28:25–26

It is bad for those who are wise in their own eyes, and who think they know a lot!

ISAIAH 5:21

If anyone wants to be proud, he should be proud of what the Lord has done. It is not what a man thinks and says of himself that is important. It is what God thinks of him.

2 CORINTHIANS 10:17–18

"How can you believe when you are always wanting honor from each other? And yet you do not look for the honor that comes from the only God."

JOHN 5:44

Pride comes before being destroyed and a proud spirit comes before a fall.

PROVERBS 16:18

God has given me His loving-favor. This helps me write these things to you. I ask each one of you not to think more of himself than he should think. Instead, think in the right way toward yourself by the faith God has given you.

ROMANS 12:3

When pride comes, then comes shame, but wisdom is with those who have no pride.

PROVERBS 11:2

Christian brothers, if a person is found doing some sin, you who are stronger Christians should lead that one back into the right way. Do not be proud as you do it. Watch yourself, because you may be tempted also. Help each other in troubles and problems. This is the kind of law Christ asks us to obey. If anyone thinks he is important when he is nothing, he is fooling himself.

GALATIANS 6:1–3

A man's pride will bring him down, but he whose spirit is without pride will receive honor.

PROVERBS 29:23

PROTECTION

God will never lead you
where His strength
cannot keep you.
BARBARA JOHNSON

The Lord of All is with us. The God of Jacob is our strong place.

PSALM 46:7

There is strong trust in the fear of the Lord, and His children will have a safe place.

PROVERBS 14:26

"When you pass through the waters, I will be with you. When you pass through the rivers, they will not flow over you. When you walk through the fire, you will not be burned. The fire will not destroy you."

ISAIAH 43:2

But the Lord has been my strong place, my God, and the rock where I am safe.

PSALM 94:22

Be a rock to me where I live, where I may always come and where I will be safe. For You are my rock and my safe place.

PSALM 71:3

Most important of all, you need a covering of faith in front of you. This is to put out the fire-arrows of the devil.

EPHESIANS 6:16

For You will make those happy who do what is right, O Lord. You will cover them all around with Your favor.

PSALM 5:12

"The Lord lives. Thanks be to my Rock. May God be honored, the Rock that saves me."

2 SAMUEL 22:47

You have also given me the covering that saves me. Your right hand holds me up. And Your care has made me great.

PSALM 18:35

The name of the Lord is a strong tower. The man who does what is right runs into it and is safe.

PROVERBS 18:10

Our soul waits for the Lord. He is our help and our safe cover.

PSALM 33:20

Every word of God has been proven true. He is a safe-covering to those who trust in Him.

PROVERBS 30:5

He will cover you with His wings. And under His wings you will be safe. He is faithful like a safe-covering and a strong wall.

PSALM 91:4

But he who listens to me will live free from danger, and he will rest easy from the fear of what is sinful.

PROVERBS 1:33

He said, "The Lord is my rock, my strong place, and the One Who sets me free. He is my God, my rock, where I go to be safe. He is my covering and the horn that saves me, my strong place where I go to be safe. You save me from being hurt. I call upon the Lord, Who should be praised. I am saved from those who hate me."

2 SAMUEL 22:2–4

The Lord is good, a safe place in times of trouble. And He knows those who come to Him to be safe.

NAHUM 1:7

Give all your cares to the Lord and He will give you strength. He will never let those who are right with Him be shaken.

PSALM 55:22

The Lord is my rock, and my safe place, and the One Who takes me out of trouble. My God is my rock, in Whom I am safe. He is my safe-covering, my saving strength, and my strong tower.

PSALM 18:2

For You are my rock and my safe place. For the honor of Your name, lead me and show me the way.

PSALM 31:3

God is our safe place and our strength. He is always our help when we are in trouble. So we will not be afraid, even if the earth is shaken and the mountains fall into the center of the sea, and even if its waters go wild with storm and the mountains shake with its action.

PSALM 46:1–3

"The God Who lives forever is your safe place. His arms are always under you. He drove away from in front of you those who hate you, and said, 'Destroy!'"

DEUTERONOMY 33:27

The Lord also keeps safe those who suffer. He is a safe place in times of trouble.

PSALM 9:9

God is our safe place and our strength. He is always our help when we are in trouble.

PSALM 46:1

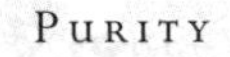

PURITY

A person of purity stands before his peers and superiors and courageously maintains his faith in God.
CINDY TRENT

Drink water from your own pool, flowing water from your own well.

PROVERBS 5:15

Destroy the desires to sin that are in you. These desires are: sex sins, anything that is not clean, a desire for sex sins, and wanting something someone else has. This is worshiping a god. It is because of these sins that the anger of God comes down on those who do not obey Him.

COLOSSIANS 3:5–6

Do not let sex sins or anything sinful be even talked about among those who belong to Christ. Do not always want everything.

EPHESIANS 5:3

"Do not do sex sins."

EXODUS 20:14

Food was meant for the stomach. The stomach needs food, but God will bring to an end both food and the stomach. The body was not meant for sex sins. It was meant to work for the Lord. The Lord is for our body. God raised the Lord from death. He will raise us from death by His power also. Do you not know that your bodies are a part of Christ Himself? Am I to take a part of Christ and make it a part of a woman who sells the use of her body? No! Never! Do you not know that a man who joins himself to a woman who sells the use of her body becomes a part of her? The Holy Writings say, "The two will become one." But if you join yourself to the Lord, you are one with Him in spirit. Have nothing to do with sex sins! Any other sin that a man does, does not hurt his own body. But the man who does a sex sin sins against his own body. Do you not know that your body is a house of God where the Holy Spirit lives? God gave you His Holy Spirit. Now you belong to God. You do not belong to yourselves. God bought you with a great price. So honor God with your body. You belong to Him.

1 Corinthians 6:13–20

Repentance

We long for revival, but revival begins with repentance.
Natalie Grant

The Lord is not slow about keeping His promise as some people think. He is waiting for you. The Lord does not want any person to be punished forever. He wants all people to be sorry for their sins and turn from them.

2 PETER 3:9

"God did not remember these times when people did not know better. But now He tells all men everywhere to be sorry for their sins and to turn from them."

ACTS 17:30

"But go and understand these words, 'I want loving-kindness and not a gift to be given.' (Hosea 6:6) For I have not come to call good people. I have come to call those who are sinners."

MATTHEW 9:13

"I tell you, it is the same way among the angels of God. If one sinner is sorry for his sins and turns from them, the angels are very happy."

LUKE 15:10

"So remember what you have received and heard. Keep it. Be sorry for your sins and turn from them. If you will not wake up, I will come as a robber. You will not know at what time I will come."

REVELATION 3:3

Do you forget about His loving-kindness to you? Do you forget how long He is waiting for you? You know that God is kind. He is trying to get you to be sorry for your sins and turn from them.

ROMANS 2:4

It will not go well for the man who hides his sins, but he who tells his sins and turns from them will be given loving-pity.

PROVERBS 28:13

Look for the Lord while He may be found. Call upon Him while He is near. Let the sinful turn from his way, and the one who does not know God turn from his thoughts. Let him turn to the Lord, and He will have loving-pity on him. Let him turn to our God, for He will for sure forgive all his sins.

ISAIAH 55:6–7

"Yet even now," says the Lord, "return to Me with all your heart, crying in sorrow and eating no food. Tear your heart and not your clothes." Return to the Lord your God, for He is full of loving-kindness and loving-pity. He is slow to anger, full of love, and ready to keep His punishment from you.

JOEL 2:12–13

He said, "The time has come. The holy nation of God is near. Be sorry for your sins, turn from them, and believe the Good News."

MARK 1:15

But you must be sorry for your sins and turn from them. You must turn to God and have your sins taken away. Then many times your soul will receive new strength from the Lord.

ACTS 3:19

The Lord is near to those who have a broken heart. And He saves those who are broken in spirit.

PSALM 34:18

"You must be sorry for this sin of yours and turn from it. Pray to the Lord that He will forgive you for having such a thought in your heart."

ACTS 8:22

Come close to God and He will come close to you. Wash your hands, you sinners. Clean up your hearts, you who want to follow the sinful ways of the world and God at the same time.

JAMES 4:8

REST

Again and again, I've found Him faithful to respond, and the closer I move to Him, the safer I feel and the better I rest.
PATSY CLAIRMONT

You rise up early, and go to bed late, and work hard for your food, all for nothing. For the Lord gives to His loved ones even while they sleep.

PSALM 127:2

I will lie down and sleep in peace. O Lord, You alone keep me safe.

PSALM 4:8

In the Holy Writings He said this about the seventh day when He made the whole world, "God rested on the seventh day from all He had made." (Genesis 2:2) ...And so God's people have a complete rest waiting for them.

HEBREWS 4:4, 9

You will not be afraid when you lie down. When you lie down, your sleep will be sweet.

PROVERBS 3:24

He who lives in the safe place of the Most High will be in the shadow of the All-powerful.

PSALM 91:1

Rest in the Lord and be willing to wait for Him. Do not trouble yourself when all goes well with the one who carries out his sinful plans.

PSALM 37:7

RIGHTEOUSNESS

We do not have to be qualified to be holy.
MADELEINE L'ENGLE

"Those who are hungry and thirsty to be right with God are happy, because they will be filled."

MATTHEW 5:6

A man who is right with God hates lies, but the actions of a sinful man are hated and he is put to shame.

PROVERBS 13:5

Do you not know that sinful men will have no place in the holy nation of God? Do not be fooled. A person who does sex sins, or who worships false gods, or who is not faithful in marriage, or men who act like women, or people who do sex sins with their own sex, will have no place in the holy nation of God.

1 CORINTHIANS 6:9

"First of all, look for the holy nation of God. Be right with Him. All these other things will be given to you also."

MATTHEW 6:33

O Lord, who may live in Your tent? Who may live on Your holy hill? He who walks without blame and does what is right and good, and speaks the truth in his heart.

PSALM 15:1–2

All of Your Word is truth, and every one of Your laws, which are always right, will last forever.

PSALM 119:160

"Then the ones right with God will shine as the sun in the holy nation of their Father. You have ears, then listen!"

MATTHEW 13:43

Those who are right with the Lord cry, and He hears them. And He takes them from all their troubles.

PSALM 34:17

Through His shining-greatness and perfect life, He has given us promises. These promises are of great worth and no amount of money can buy them. Through these promises you can have God's own life in you now that you have gotten away from the sinful things of the world which came from wrong desires of the flesh.

2 PETER 1:4

But if you obey his voice and do all that I say, then I will hate those who hate you and fight against those who fight against you.

EXODUS 23:22

If we tell Him our sins, He is faithful and we can depend on Him to forgive us of our sins. He will make our lives clean from all sin.

1 JOHN 1:9

Let those who love the Lord hate what is bad. For He keeps safe the souls of His faithful ones. He takes them away from the hand of the sinful. Light is spread like seed for those who are right and good, and joy for the pure in heart.

PSALM 97:10–11

"Be faithful in obeying the Lord your God. Be careful to keep all His Laws which I tell you today. And the Lord your God will set you high above all the nations of the earth."

DEUTERONOMY 28:1

The eyes of the Lord are on those who do what is right and good. His ears are open to their cry.

PSALM 34:15

The Lord will not let those who are right with Him go hungry, but He puts to one side the desire of the sinful.

PROVERBS 10:3

Then your light will break out like the early morning, and you will soon be healed. Your right and good works will go before you. And the shining-greatness of the Lord will keep watch behind you.

Isaiah 58:8

"Those who have it very hard for doing right are happy, because the holy nation of heaven is theirs."

Matthew 5:10

He who follows what is right and loving and kind finds life, right-standing with God and honor.

Proverbs 21:21

Know that the Lord has set apart him who is God-like for Himself. The Lord hears when I call to Him.

Psalm 4:3

"Then He will say to them, 'For sure, I tell you, because you did not do it to one of the least of these, you did not do it to Me.' These will go to the place where they will be punished forever. But those right with God will have life that lasts forever."

Matthew 25:45–46

The man who is right and good will be glad in the Lord and go to Him to be safe. All those whose hearts are right will give Him praise.

Psalm 64:10

Salvation

Christ has made all things right. I had nothing to do but accept it as a free gift from Him.
HANNAH WHITALL SMITH

For if a man belongs to Christ, he is a new person. The old life is gone. New life has begun.

2 CORINTHIANS 5:17

My dear children, I am writing this to you so you will not sin. But if anyone does sin, there is One Who will go between him and the Father. He is Jesus Christ, the One Who is right with God. He paid for our sins with His own blood. He did not pay for ours only, but for the sins of the whole world.

1 JOHN 2:1–2

It is good when you pray like this. It pleases God Who is the One Who saves. He wants all people to be saved from the punishment of sin. He wants them to come to know the truth.

1 TIMOTHY 2:3–4

He gave the right and the power to become children of God to those who received Him. He gave this to those who put their trust in His name. These children of God were not born of blood and of flesh and of man's desires, but they were born of God.

JOHN 1:12–13

"He who puts his trust in the Son has life that lasts forever. He who does not put his trust in the Son will not have life, but the anger of God is on him."

JOHN 3:36

"There is no way to be saved from the punishment of sin through anyone else. For there is no other name under heaven given to men by which we can be saved."

ACTS 4:12

But God, the One Who saves, showed how kind He was and how He loved us by saving us from the punishment of sin. It was not because we worked to be right with God. It was because of His loving-kindness that He washed our sins away. At the same time He gave us new life when the Holy Spirit came into our lives. God gave the Holy Spirit to fill our lives through Jesus Christ, the One Who saves.

TITUS 3:4–6

Christ never sinned but God put our sin on Him. Then we are made right with God because of what Christ has done for us.

2 CORINTHIANS 5:21

I want to please everyone in all that I do. I am not thinking of myself. I want to do what is best for them so they may be saved from the punishment of sin.

1 CORINTHIANS 10:33

Jesus said to him, "For sure, I tell you, unless a man is born again, he cannot see the holy nation of God." Nicodemus said to Him, "How can a man be born when he is old?

How can he get into his mother's body and be born the second time?" Jesus answered, "For sure, I tell you, unless a man is born of water and of the Spirit of God, he cannot get into the holy nation of God. Whatever is born of the flesh is flesh. Whatever is born of the Spirit is spirit. "Do not be surprised that I said to you, 'You must be born again.' "

JOHN 3:3–7

SCRIPTURE

How much of a calm and gentle spirit you achieve, then, will depend on how regularly and consistently, persistently and obediently you partake of the Word of God, your spiritual food.
SHIRLEY RICE

Let the teaching of Christ and His words keep on living in you. These make your lives rich and full of wisdom. Keep on teaching and helping each other. Sing the Songs of David and the church songs and the songs of heaven with hearts full of thanks to God.

COLOSSIANS 3:16

Your Word have I hid in my heart, that I may not sin against You.

PSALM 119:11

Your Word is a lamp to my feet and a light to my path.
PSALM 119:105

You have known the Holy Writings since you were a child. They are able to give you wisdom that leads to being saved from the punishment of sin by putting your trust in Christ Jesus.

2 TIMOTHY 3:15

"Keep these words of mine in your heart and in your soul. Tie them as something special to see upon your hand and on your forehead between your eyes. Teach them to your children. Talk about them when you sit in your house and when you walk on the road and when you lie down and when you get up."

DEUTERONOMY 11:18–19

God's Word is living and powerful. It is sharper than a sword that cuts both ways. It cuts straight into where the soul and spirit meet and it divides them. It cuts into the joints and bones. It tells what the heart is thinking about and what it wants to do.

HEBREWS 4:12

You should remember the words that were spoken before by the holy early preachers. Do not forget the teaching of the Lord, the One Who saves. This was given to you by your missionaries.

2 PETER 3:2

"So My Word which goes from My mouth will not return to Me empty. It will do what I want it to do, and will carry out My plan well."

ISAIAH 55:11

Long ago God spoke to our early fathers in many different ways. He spoke through the early preachers. But in these last days He has spoken to us through His Son. God gave His Son everything. It was by His Son that God made the world.

HEBREWS 1:1–2

This book of the Law must not leave your mouth. Think about it day and night, so you may be careful to do all that is written in it. Then all will go well with you. You will receive many good things.

JOSHUA 1:8

The early preachers wondered at what time or to what person this would happen. The Spirit of Christ in them was talking to them and told them to write about how Christ would suffer and about His shining-greatness later on. They knew these things would not happen during the time they lived but while you are living many years later. These are the very things that were told to you by those who preached the Good News. The Holy Spirit Who was sent from heaven gave them power and they told of things that even the angels would like to know about.

1 PETER 1:11–12

SEEKING GOD

For it is impossible to be in the presence of Jesus
and not be changed.
JOANNA WEAVER

"First of all, look for the holy nation of God. Be right with Him. All these other things will be given to you also."

MATTHEW 6:33

Plant what is right and good for yourselves. Gather the fruit of lasting love. Break up your ground that has not been plowed. For it is time to look for the Lord, until He comes and pours His saving power on you.

HOSEA 10:12

Have joy in His holy name. Let the heart of those who look to the Lord be glad. Look to the Lord and ask for His strength. Look to Him all the time.

1 CHRONICLES 16:10–11

You will look for Me and find Me, when you look for Me with all your heart.

JEREMIAH 29:13

One thing I have asked from the Lord, that I will look for: that I may live in the house of the Lord all the days of my life, to look upon the beauty of the Lord, and to worship in His holy house.

PSALM 27:4

My soul has a desire for You in the night. Yes, my spirit within me looks for You in the morning. For when you punish the earth, the people of the world learn what is right and good.

ISAIAH 26:9

"I say to you, ask, and what you ask for will be given to you. Look, and what you are looking for you will find. Knock, and the door you are knocking on will be opened to you."

LUKE 11:9

So I have come out to meet you, to look for you, and I have found you.

PROVERBS 7:15

But from there you will look for the Lord your God. And you will find Him if you look for Him with all your heart and soul.

DEUTERONOMY 4:29

Look for the Lord and live.

AMOS 5:6

If then you have been raised with Christ, keep looking for the good things of heaven. This is where Christ is seated on the right side of God.

COLOSSIANS 3:1

The young lions suffer want and hunger. But they who look for the Lord will not be without any good thing.

PSALM 34:10

If My people who are called by My name put away their pride and pray, and look for My face, and turn from their sinful ways, then I will hear from heaven. I will forgive their sin, and will heal their land.

2 CHRONICLES 7:14

"Instead, go after the holy nation of God. Then all these other things will be given to you."

LUKE 12:31

SELF-CONTROL

Rules for proper behavior keep us from getting hurt. We risk our own life and the lives of others when we give in to our desires, whatever they might be.
LINDA BARTLETT

Then Pilate said to Him, "Do You not hear all these things they are saying against You?" Jesus did not say a word. The leader was much surprised and wondered about it.

MATTHEW 27:13–14

Michael was one of the head angels. He argued with the devil about the body of Moses. But Michael would not speak sharp words to the devil, saying he was guilty. He said, "The Lord speaks sharp words to you."

JUDE 9

These things are all a part of the Christian life to which you have been called. Christ suffered for us. This shows us we are to follow in His steps. He never sinned. No lie or bad talk ever came from His lips. When people spoke against Him, He never spoke back. When He suffered from what people did to Him, He did not try to pay them back. He left it in the hands of the One Who is always right in judging.

1 PETER 2:21–23

Have you found honey? Eat only what you need, or you may become filled with it and spit it up.

PROVERBS 25:16

Love does not give up. Love is kind. Love is not jealous. Love does not put itself up as being important. Love has no pride. Love does not do the wrong thing. Love never thinks of itself. Love does not get angry. Love does not remember the suffering that comes from being hurt by someone.

1 CORINTHIANS 13:4–5

Let all people see how gentle you are. The Lord is coming again soon.

PHILIPPIANS 4:5

Keep awake! Do not sleep like others. Watch and keep your minds awake to what is happening. People sleep at night. Those who get drunk do it at night.

1 THESSALONIANS 5:6–7

If the ruler becomes angry with you, do not back away. If you are quiet, much wrong-doing may be put aside.

ECCLESIASTES 10:4

We must act all the time as if it were day. Keep away from wild parties and do not be drunk. Keep yourself free from sex sins and bad actions. Do not fight or be jealous. Let every part of you belong to the Lord Jesus Christ. Do not allow your weak thoughts to lead you into sinful actions.

ROMANS 13:13–14

Do your best to add holy living to your faith. Then add to this a better understanding. As you have a better understanding, be able to say no when you need to. Do not give up. And as you wait and do not give up, live God-like.

2 Peter 1:5–6

Older men are to be quiet and to be careful how they act. They are to be the boss over their own desires. Their faith and love are to stay strong and they are not to give up. Teach older women to be quiet and to be careful how they act also. They are not to go around speaking bad things about others or things that are not true. They are not to be chained by strong drink. They should teach what is good.

Titus 2:2–3

Everyone who runs in a race does many things so his body will be strong. He does it to get a crown that will soon be worth nothing, but we work for a crown that will last forever.

1 Corinthians 9:25

We are taught to have nothing to do with that which is against God. We are to have nothing to do with the desires of this world. We are to be wise and to be right with God. We are to live God-like lives in this world.

Titus 2:12

I keep working over my body. I make it obey me. I do this because I am afraid that after I have preached the Good News to others, I myself might be put aside.

1 Corinthians 9:27

Church helpers must also be good men and act so people will respect them. They must speak the truth. They must not get drunk. They must not have a love for money.

1 TIMOTHY 3:8

Do you not know that sinful men will have no place in the holy nation of God? Do not be fooled. A person who does sex sins, or who worships false gods, or who is not faithful in marriage, or men who act like women, or people who do sex sins with their own sex, will have no place in the holy nation of God. Also those who steal, or those who always want to get more of everything, or who get drunk, or who say bad things about others, or take things that are not theirs, will have no place in the holy nation of God. Some of you were like that. But now your sins are washed away. You were set apart for God-like living to do His work. You were made right with God through our Lord Jesus Christ by the Spirit of our God.

1 CORINTHIANS 6:9–11

If you do what your sinful old selves want you to do, you will die in sin. But if, through the power of the Holy Spirit, you destroy those actions to which the body can be led, you will have life.

ROMANS 8:13

Sin

It is the very nature of sin to prevent man from meditating on spiritual things.
Mary Martha Sherwood

For if a man belongs to Christ, he is a new person. The old life is gone. New life has begun.
2 Corinthians 5:17

"I will show loving-kindness to them and forgive their sins. I will remember their sins no more." (Jeremiah 31:31–34)
Hebrews 8:12

If we live in the light as He is in the light, we share what we have in God with each other. And the blood of Jesus Christ, His Son, makes our lives clean from all sin.
1 John 1:7

"Come now, let us think about this together," says the Lord. "Even though your sins are bright red, they will be as white as snow. Even though they are dark red, they will be like wool.
Isaiah 1:18

"This is My blood of the New Way of Worship which is given for many. It is given so the sins of many can be forgiven."
Matthew 26:28

But He was hurt for our wrong-doing. He was crushed for our sins. He was punished so we would have peace. He was beaten so we would be healed. All of us like sheep have gone the wrong way. Each of us has turned to his own way. And the Lord has put on Him the sin of us all.

ISAIAH 53:5–6

My dear children, I am writing this to you so you will not sin. But if anyone does sin, there is One Who will go between him and the Father. He is Jesus Christ, the One Who is right with God. He paid for our sins with His own blood. He did not pay for ours only, but for the sins of the whole world.

1 JOHN 2:1–2

"All the early preachers spoke of this. Everyone who puts his trust in Christ will have his sins forgiven through His name."

ACTS 10:43

What I say is true and all the world should receive it. Christ Jesus came into the world to save sinners from their sin and I am the worst sinner.

1 TIMOTHY 1:15

He carried our sins in His own body when He died on a cross. In doing this, we may be dead to sin and alive to all that is right and good. His wounds have healed you!

1 PETER 2:24

He has taken our sins from us as far as the east is from the west.

PSALM 103:12

We know that our old life, our old sinful self, was nailed to the cross with Christ. And so the power of sin that held us was destroyed. Sin is no longer our boss. When a man is dead, he is free from the power of sin.

ROMANS 6:6–7

He gave Himself to die for our sins. He did this so we could be saved from this sinful world. This is what God wanted Him to do.

GALATIANS 1:4

SINCERITY

Speaking beautifully is little to the purpose unless one lives beautifully.
ELIZABETH PRENTISS

How happy is the man whose sin the Lord does not hold against him, and in whose spirit there is nothing false.

PSALM 32:2

No lie has come from their mouths. They are without blame.

REVELATION 14:5

Get your minds ready for good use. Keep awake. Set your hope now and forever on the loving-favor to be given you when Jesus Christ comes again.

1 PETER 1:13

Because we are men of the day, let us keep our minds awake. Let us cover our chests with faith and love. Let us cover our heads with the hope of being saved.

1 THESSALONIANS 5:8

As new babies want milk, you should want to drink the pure milk which is God's Word so you will grow up and be saved from the punishment of sin.

1 PETER 2:2

May God give loving-favor to all who love our Lord Jesus Christ with a love that never gets weak.

EPHESIANS 6:24

We are not like others. They preach God's Word to make money. We are men of truth and have been sent by God. We speak God's Word with Christ's power. All the time God sees us.

2 CORINTHIANS 2:17

"So fear the Lord. Serve Him in faith and truth. Put away the gods your fathers served on the other side of the river and in Egypt. Serve the Lord."

JOSHUA 24:14

We want to see our teaching help you have a true love that comes from a pure heart. Such love comes from a heart that says we are not guilty and from a faith that does not pretend.

1 TIMOTHY 1:5

Be sure your love is true love. Hate what is sinful. Hold on to whatever is good.

ROMANS 12:9

You have made your souls pure by obeying the truth through the Holy Spirit. This has given you a true love for the Christians. Let it be a true love from the heart.

1 Peter 1:22

I am happy to say this. Whatever we did in this world, and for sure when we were with you, we were honest and had pure desires. We did not trust in human wisdom. Our power came from God's loving-favor.

2 Corinthians 1:12

You remember what we said to you was true. We had no wrong desire in teaching you. We did not try to fool you. God has allowed us to be trusted with the Good News. Because of this, we preach it to please God, not man. God tests and proves our hearts. You know we never used smooth-sounding words. God knows we never tried to get money from you by preaching.

1 Thessalonians 2:3–5

Bread with yeast in it is like being full of sin and hate. Let us eat this supper together with bread that has no yeast in it. This bread is pure and true.

1 Corinthians 5:8

Put out of your life hate and lying. Do not pretend to be someone you are not. Do not always want something someone else has. Do not say bad things about other people.

1 Peter 2:1

I pray that you will know what is the very best. I pray that you will be true and without blame until the day Christ comes again.

PHILIPPIANS 1:10

I am not saying that you must do this, but I have told you how others have helped. This is a way to prove how true your love is.

2 CORINTHIANS 8:8

SOBRIETY

"Abstain," says God.
He doesn't say, "Be careful" or "Pray about it."
He says, "Abstain! Run from it!
Don't touch it!
Have nothing to do with it!"
Stay pure and blameless.
If you don't, God will suffer most of all.
ANNE ORTLUND

(The things your sinful old self wants to do are:) Wanting something someone else has, killing other people, using strong drink, wild parties, and all things like these. I told you before and I am telling you again that those who do these things will have no place in the holy nation of God.

GALATIANS 5:21

"Their sinful ways and both old and new wine take away My people's understanding."

HOSEA 4:11

He will be great in the sight of the Lord and will never drink wine or any strong drink. Even from his birth, he will be filled with the Holy Spirit.

LUKE 1:15

Wine makes people act in a foolish way. Strong drink starts fights. Whoever is fooled by it is not wise.

PROVERBS 20:1

It is bad for those who get up early in the morning to run after strong drink! It is bad for those who stay up late in the evening that they may get drunk!

ISAIAH 5:11

They have drawn names to see who would get My people. They have traded a boy for a woman who sells the use of her body. And they have sold a girl for wine to drink.

JOEL 3:3

Who has trouble? Who has sorrow? Who is fighting? Who is complaining? Who is hurt without a reason? Who has eyes that have become red? Those who stay a long time over wine. Those who go to taste mixed wine. Do not look at wine when it is red, when it shines in the cup, when it is smooth in going down. In the end it bites like a snake. It stings like the bite of a snake with poison.

PROVERBS 23:29–32

So be careful not to drink wine or strong drink. Do not eat anything that is unclean.

JUDGES 13:4

"It is bad for him who makes his neighbors drink, mixing in his poison to make them drunk, so he can look on their shame!"

HABAKKUK 2:15

"Watch yourselves! Do not let yourselves be loaded down with too much eating and strong drink. Do not be troubled with the cares of this life. If you do, that day will come on you without you knowing it."

LUKE 21:34

They are like thorns that tie themselves together, like those who are drunk with strong drink. They are destroyed like dry grass.

NAHUM 1:10

For the man who drinks too much or eats too much will become poor, and much sleep will dress a man in torn clothes.

PROVERBS 23:21

STRENGTH

We must continue to ask God for wisdom and insight and for the strength to persevere. He will cause us to rise up and fly like eagles, walking and not fainting.
NORMA SMALLEY

For the eyes of the Lord move over all the earth so that He may give strength to those whose whole heart is given to Him.

2 CHRONICLES 16:9

Both riches and honor come from You. You rule over all. Power and strength are in Your hand. The power is in Your hand to make great and to give strength to all.

1 CHRONICLES 29:12

This is the last thing I want to say: Be strong with the Lord's strength.

EPHESIANS 6:10

He gives strength to the weak. And He gives power to him who has little strength.

ISAIAH 40:29

Wait for the Lord. Be strong. Let your heart be strong. Yes, wait for the Lord.

PSALM 27:14

The Lord will give strength to His people. The Lord will give His people peace.

PSALM 29:11

The Lord is my rock, and my safe place, and the One Who takes me out of trouble. My God is my rock, in Whom I am safe. He is my safe-covering, my saving strength, and my strong tower.

PSALM 18:2

I know how to get along with little and how to live when I have much. I have learned the secret of being happy at all times. If I am full of food and have all I need, I am happy. If I am hungry and need more, I am happy. I can do all things because Christ gives me the strength.

PHILIPPIANS 4:12–13

But they who wait upon the Lord will get new strength. They will rise up with wings like eagles. They will run and not get tired. They will walk and not become weak.

ISAIAH 40:31

My body and my heart may grow weak, but God is the strength of my heart and all I need forever.

PSALM 73:26

But the one who is right with God will hold to his way. And he who has clean hands will become stronger and stronger.

JOB 17:9

Then your lives will please the Lord. You will do every kind of good work, and you will know more about God. I pray that God's great power will make you strong, and that you will have joy as you wait and do not give up.

COLOSSIANS 1:10–11

O God, You are honored with fear as You come from Your holy place. The God of Israel Himself gives strength and power to His people. Honor and thanks be to God!

PSALM 68:35

He answered me, "I am all you need. I give you My loving-favor. My power works best in weak people." I am happy to be weak and have troubles so I can have Christ's power in me.

2 CORINTHIANS 12:9

But we have power over all these things through Jesus Who loves us so much.

ROMANS 8:37

TEMPTATION

Temptations come, as a general rule, when they are sought.
MARGARET OLIPHANT

The man who does not give up when tests come is happy. After the test is over, he will receive the crown of life. God has promised this to those who love Him. When you are tempted to do wrong, do not say, "God is tempting me." God cannot be tempted. He will never tempt anyone. A man is tempted to do wrong when he lets himself be led by what his bad thoughts tell him to do.

JAMES 1:12–14

"I will keep you from the time of trouble. The time to test everyone is about to come to the whole world. I will do this because you have listened to Me and have waited long and have not given up."

REVELATION 3:10

"'Do not let us be tempted, but keep us from sin. *Your nation is holy. You have power and shining-greatness forever. Let it be so.'"

MATTHEW 6:13

But the Lord knows how to help men who are right with God when they are tempted. He also knows how to keep the sinners suffering for their wrong-doing until the day they stand before God Who will judge them.

2 PETER 2:9

"Watch and pray so that you will not be tempted. Man's spirit is willing, but the body does not have the power to do it."

MATTHEW 26:41

When He got there, He said to them, "Pray that you will not be tempted."

LUKE 22:40

You have never been tempted to sin in any different way than other people. God is faithful. He will not allow you to be tempted more than you can take. But when you are tempted, He will make a way for you to keep from falling into sin.

1 CORINTHIANS 10:13

Truth

If we are Christians, we have committed ourselves to the Lord Jesus Christ who said, "I am the Truth." In giving ourselves to Him, we dedicate ourselves to the truth not only about Him but about ourselves.
PAMELA HOOVER HEIM

"God is Spirit. Those who worship Him must worship Him in spirit and in truth."

JOHN 4:24

"He is the Spirit of Truth. The world cannot receive Him. It does not see Him or know Him. You know Him because He lives with you and will be in you."

JOHN 14:17

Buy truth, and do not sell it. Get wisdom and teaching and understanding.

PROVERBS 23:23

For the Lord is good. His loving-kindness lasts forever. And He is faithful to all people and to all their children-to-come.

PSALM 100:5

Jesus said, "I am the Way and the Truth and the Life. No one can go to the Father except by Me."

JOHN 14:6

The Rock! His work is perfect. All His ways are right and fair. A God Who is faithful and without sin, right and good is He.

DEUTERONOMY 32:4

Christian brothers, keep your minds thinking about whatever is true, whatever is respected, whatever is right, whatever is pure, whatever can be loved, and whatever is well thought of. If there is anything good and worth giving thanks for, think about these things.

PHILIPPIANS 4:8

"You will know the truth and the truth will make you free."

JOHN 8:32

Anyone who has good things come to him in the land will have good things come to him by the God of truth. And he who makes a promise in the land will promise by the God of truth. The troubles of the past are forgotten, and are hidden from My eyes.

ISAIAH 65:16

For the Word of the Lord is right. He is faithful in all He does.

PSALM 33:4

"I set Myself apart to be holy for them. Then they may be made holy by the truth."

JOHN 17:19

These are the things you are to do: Speak the truth to one another. Judge with truth so there will be peace within your gates.

ZECHARIAH 8:16

The Law was given through Moses, but loving-favor and truth came through Jesus Christ.

JOHN 1:17

UNDERSTANDING

Yearn to understand first and to be understood second.
BECA LEWIS ALLEN

Happy is the man who finds wisdom, and the man who gets understanding. For it is better than getting silver and fine gold. She is worth more than stones of great worth. Nothing you can wish for compares with her.

PROVERBS 3:13–15

Then you will understand the fear of the Lord, and find what is known of God. For the Lord gives wisdom. Much learning and understanding come from His mouth.

PROVERBS 2:5–6

They will not hurt or destroy in all My holy mountain. For the earth will be as full of much learning from the Lord as the seas are full of water. In that day the nations will turn to the One from the family of Jesse. He will be honored by the people as someone special to see. And His place of rest will be full of His shining-greatness.

ISAIAH 11:9–10

For wisdom will come into your heart. And much learning will be pleasing to your soul. Good thinking will keep you safe. Understanding will watch over you.

PROVERBS 2:10–12

Are you strong because you belong to Christ? Does His love comfort you? Do you have joy by being as one in sharing the Holy Spirit? Do you have loving-kindness and pity for each other?

PHILIPPIANS 2:1–2

The tongue of the wise uses much learning in a good way, but the mouth of fools speaks in a foolish way.

PROVERBS 15:2

Your throne stands on what is right and fair. Loving-kindness and truth go before You.

PSALM 89:14

When I was a child, I spoke like a child. I thought like a child. I understood like a child. Now I am a man. I do not act like a child anymore.

1 CORINTHIANS 13:11

Wisdom is found on the lips of him who has understanding, but a stick is for the back of him who has no understanding.

PROVERBS 10:13

"And He said to man, 'See, the fear of the Lord, that is wisdom. And to turn away from sin is understanding.' "
Job 28:28

Wisdom is with old men, and understanding with long life. "With God are wisdom and strength. Wise words and understanding belong to Him."
Job 12:12–13

Wisdom rests in the heart of one who has understanding, but what is in the heart of fools is made known.
Proverbs 14:33

"But let him who speaks with pride speak about this, that he understands and knows Me, that I am the Lord who shows loving-kindness and does what is fair and right and good on earth. For I find joy in these things," says the Lord.
Jeremiah 9:24

Sinful men do not understand what is right and fair, but those who look to the Lord understand all things.
Proverbs 28:5

The Holy Writings say, "No eye has ever seen or no ear has ever heard or no mind has ever thought of the wonderful things God has made ready for those who love Him." (Isaiah 64:4; 65:17) God has shown these things to us through His Holy Spirit. It is the Holy Spirit Who looks into all things, even the secrets of God, and shows them to us. Who can know the things about a man, except a man's own spirit that is in him? It is the same with God. Who can understand Him except the Holy Spirit?
1 Corinthians 2:9–11

A foolish way is joy to him who has no wisdom, but a man of understanding walks straight.

PROVERBS 15:21

Do your best to add holy living to your faith. Then add to this a better understanding. As you have a better understanding, be able to say no when you need to. Do not give up. And as you wait and do not give up, live God-like. As you live God-like, be kind to Christian brothers and love them. If you have all these things and keep growing in them, they will keep you from being of no use and from having no fruit when it comes to knowing our Lord Jesus Christ.

2 PETER 1:5–8

Make me understand the way of Your Law so I will talk about Your great works.

PSALM 119:27

The rich man is wise in his own eyes, but the poor man who has understanding sees through him.

PROVERBS 28:11

Teach me what I should know to be right and fair for I believe in Your Law.

PSALM 119:66

The mind of him who has understanding looks for much learning, but the mouth of fools feeds on foolish ways.

PROVERBS 15:14

One person is given the gift of teaching words of wisdom. Another person is given the gift of teaching what he has learned and knows. These gifts are by the same Holy Spirit.

1 CORINTHIANS 12:8

Unity

The Word tells us that He has called His children to be one with Him and with each other. In order for His will to be realized, we must first unite. To unite simply means to join.
Katheryn Boone

Do two men walk together unless they have made an agreement?

Amos 3:3

See, how good and how pleasing it is for brothers to live together as one!

Psalm 133:1

Live in peace with each other. Do not act or think with pride. Be happy to be with poor people. Keep yourself from thinking you are so wise.

Romans 12:16

Now the God Who helps you not to give up and gives you strength will help you think so you can please each other as Christ Jesus did. Then all of you together can thank the God and Father of our Lord Jesus Christ.

Romans 15:5–6

Look for peace and go after it.

1 Peter 3:11

Christian brothers, I ask you with all my heart in the name of the Lord Jesus Christ to agree among yourselves. Do not be divided into little groups. Think and act as if you all had the same mind.

1 CORINTHIANS 1:10

WISDOM

Learning is not attained by chance; it must be sought for with ardor and attended to with diligence.
ABIGAIL ADAMS

He who obeys the king's law will have no trouble, for a wise heart knows the right time and way.

ECCLESIASTES 8:5

Do not be foolish. Understand what the Lord wants you to do.

EPHESIANS 5:17

"Whoever hears these words of Mine and does them, will be like a wise man who built his house on rock. The rain came down. The water came up. The wind blew and hit the house. The house did not fall because it was built on rock."

MATTHEW 7:24–25

He who hates his neighbor does not think well, but a man of understanding keeps quiet.

PROVERBS 11:12

A wise man sees sin and hides himself, but the foolish go on, and are punished for it.

PROVERBS 22:3

The Lord built the earth by wisdom. He built the heavens by understanding. By what He knows, the seas were broken up and water falls from the sky. My son, do not allow them to leave your eyes. Keep perfect wisdom and careful thinking.

PROVERBS 3:19–21

A wise man hides how much learning he has, but the heart of fools makes known their foolish way.

PROVERBS 12:23

The one who is easy to fool believes everything, but the wise man looks where he goes.

PROVERBS 14:15

To get wisdom is much better than getting gold. To get understanding should be chosen instead of silver.

PROVERBS 16:16

He who listens to the Word will find good, and happy is he who trusts in the Lord. The wise in heart will be called understanding. And to speak in a pleasing way helps people know what you say is right.

PROVERBS 16:20–21

Whoever is wise, let him understand these things and know them. For the ways of the Lord are right, and those who are right and good will follow them, but sinners will not follow them.

HOSEA 14:9

My son, listen to my words. Turn your ear to my sayings. Do not let them leave your eyes. Keep them in the center of your heart. For they are life to those who find them, and healing to their whole body.

PROVERBS 4:20–22

The teaching of the wise is a well of life, to save one from the nets of death. Good understanding wins favor, but the way of the sinful is hard.

PROVERBS 13:14–15

Everyone knows you have obeyed the teaching you received. I am happy with you because of this. But I want you to be wise about good things and pure about sinful things.

ROMANS 16:19

Those who are wise will shine like the bright heavens. And those who lead many to do what is right and good will shine like the stars forever and ever.

DANIEL 12:3

Strength and wisdom are with Him. Both the fool and the one who fools him belong to God. He takes wisdom away from leaders and makes fools of judges.

JOB 12:16–17

My son, eat honey, for it is good. Yes, the honey from the comb is sweet to your taste. Know that wisdom is like this to your soul. If you find it, there will be a future, and your hope will not be cut off.

PROVERBS 24:13–14

He will be for you what is sure and faithful for your times, with much saving power, wisdom and learning. The fear of the Lord is worth much.

Isaiah 33:6

I will show you and teach you in the way you should go. I will tell you what to do with My eye upon you.

Psalm 32:8

If you do not have wisdom, ask God for it. He is always ready to give it to you and will never say you are wrong for asking.

James 1:5

We speak wisdom to full-grown Christians. This wisdom is not from this world or from the leaders of today. They die and their wisdom dies with them. What we preach is God's wisdom. It was a secret until now. God planned for us to have this honor before the world began. None of the world leaders understood this wisdom. If they had, they would not have put Christ up on a cross to die. He is the Lord of shining-greatness.

1 Corinthians 2:6–8

The person who thinks he knows all the answers still has a lot to learn.

1 Corinthians 8:2

For wisdom keeps one from danger just as money keeps one from danger. But the good thing about much learning is that wisdom keeps alive those who have it.

Ecclesiastes 7:12